JESUS'
SURPRISING
STRATEGY

A mandate and a means
for city transformation

David Drum

D0677529

Dear 2013
Covenant participant:

There are several ways that *Jesus' Surprising Strategy* might aid your city's transformation efforts:

- Jesus prayed for your work! You'll find great encouragement here.
- The biblical basis, particularly drawing from John 17, 1 Corinthians 12, and Ephesians 4, will provide common language to further unify and mobilize the body of Christ in your city.
- Over and over again, we hear that city transformation efforts rise and fall on the strength of relationships. *Jesus' Surprising Strategy* aims at that target.
- Many aspects of this book grew out of citywide pastors' prayer summits. If your city has been blessed with such summits, past participants will find much here they can resonate with. Perhaps some would be willing to read and discuss it together. Bulk order discounts are available.
- Already-existing networks of pastors and leaders are another key audience.
- Small groups within congregations can work through the book together. A *free* eight week small group guide is on the book website: www.JesusSurprisingStrategy.com. Again, bulk discounts of the book are available.
- Small groups organized around domains or other networks would also benefit from the practical implementation strategies contained in the book and small group guide.

Thanks so much! I've set up a separate email address for book correspondence – jss@4tucson.com.

Dave Drum

What they're saying about *Jesus' Surprising Strategy*

Do you have a desire to have more people in your neighborhood, community, city, or county know Jesus? Do you want them to have an attractive opportunity to see and hear the good news? Jesus has that same desire. Do you have a strategy to see this take place? Jesus does. Does your strategy match Jesus' strategy? Jesus' strategy may be surprising, but it is not hidden. God has given my friend, David Drum, a unique history and heart to not only know this strategy, but also to live it and to see it implemented in his city. *Jesus' Surprising Strategy* is an opportunity for you to look over Dave's shoulder and see Jesus at work in his own life, his congregation, and his city. But it doesn't have to stop there. In fact, it shouldn't! *Jesus' Surprising Strategy* must be implemented in as many places as possible. My encouragement is that you read it, ponder it, implement it, and share it!

Dennis Fuqua
President, International Renewal Ministries

In post-Christendom America, we need fresh guidance for how to be the Church of Jesus Christ. Dave Drum unpacks a biblical base for, and invites us to dive into, a seldom pursued expression of Christianity: citywide interaction and unity among Christians and their churches. If we who follow Christ are to have an impact in our culture we will need to actually demonstrate we are on the same page. This book will help that happen.

Paul Spaulding
Pastoral Certification Coordinator
Lutheran Congregations in Mission for Christ

Jesus' Surprising Strategy is just that—a surprisingly simple strategy for making the Kingdom of God visible in a city…in your community. Dave builds a case for unity not just for unity's sake but as the Jesus-given way of making the invisible Kingdom of God present and visible in a community.

Eric Swanson
Leadership Network
Co-author of *To Transform a City:
Whole Church, Whole Gospel, Whole City*

Unity. We know we are called to it. We know we haven't been good at it. We know we will need to sacrifice ingrown ways to achieve it. A good friend, David Drum, can help us with the whole process. He's not only writing about it—he's doing it! I've known Dave as a gifted communicator for many years. Get his book and you'll agree.

Paul Anderson
Former Director, Lutheran Renewal

I'm so pleased that Dave Drum wrote *Jesus' Surprising Strategy.* It has been my prayer for my entire Christian life that the body of Christ would fulfill the prayer of Jesus in John 17, laying aside their differences to become a bright shining light to the world. This book offers a clear call to that purpose and gives us once again the opportunity to return to the heart of God, demonstrating His magnificent love to a hurting and dying world in need of JESUS.

Hal Sacks
President, BridgeBuilders International

Our world has been filled with conflict since the Garden of Eden. David Drum has hit on one of the key chords that Jesus gave us to play in the world. Those of us that are Christians are to be unified, one in Him, and bring the ministry of reconciliation. David has that heart and has done an excellent job of expressing this desire and mission in this book.

Doug Martin
President, General Manager
Good News Radio Broadcasting

When we pray, we ask Jesus to answer our prayers. What would you think about being the answer to a prayer Jesus prayed? I would recommend this book to anyone interested in understanding the scriptural basis for churches working together for city transformation. Jesus prayed that we would comprehend and use His strategy. After reading this book, you may want to be the answer to Jesus' prayer in your city.

Mark Harris
Founder and Executive Director, 4Tucson

The cities, towns and villages across our land need the influence and loving care of a dynamic church. It is a church that is composed of many congregations working together to become the living, breathing example of Christ-hope and solution. Pastor Drum reveals in practical ways how Jesus' prayer for unity in John 17 can come to fruition today. I highly recommend this book for churches that have a passion for their cities and desire to work practically with other congregations. This book doesn't just talk about Christian unity, but is a practical guide in how to accomplish it.

Rick Leis
Pastor, Connections Vineyard,
and Founder, Coalition of Prayer Network

David Drum has written a comprehensive and practical book on unity in the body of Christ. For all of those that pursue unity, this book will quickly resonate in your spirit. Whether you consider yourself a theologian or layperson, you will be blessed by this anointed labor of love.

Otis Brown
Pastor, Siloam Freewill Church
Acting President, Interdenominational Ministerial Alliance

Dave Drum, whose work in the city of Tucson has been a John 17 testimony, reminds us in his book *Jesus' Surprising Strategy* of the priority and urgency of Christ's prayer. This informative book outlines the practical steps which lead to the unifying of the Body of Christ as spoken of in John 17. After reading Dave's book, you will either discover or rediscover two things: One, the Head of the church has placed in each believer the capacity to build bridges that lead to the unifying of the Body of Christ. And two, you will discover that God is bringing you personally to a point of decision (investor or cheerleader).

Warren Anderson Jr.
Senior Pastor, Living Water Ministries Church

Jesus' Surprising Strategy is right on target and desperately needed in our world today. Dave Drum has captured the heart of Jesus' prayer and strategy to bring the Kingdom of God to our communities as it is in the community of heaven. Not only does Dave write in a captivating manner, but he also is living out the very prayer that Jesus prayed! This is not just theory and theology—it is being lived out in our city and I have the honor of watching Dave model and fulfill Jesus' prayer for unity and transformation.

Glen Elliott
Senior Pastor, Pantano Christian Church

Dave's book on unity is a must read. In this book, you find a great foundation for Christian unity—one of the main missions that Christ calls us to in our lives. Through practical examples and sound theology, Dave points the way to unity in the body of Christ. In a culture as individualistic as ours, unity is often countercultural and part of the transforming work of God so the church can truly represent Christ to the world through its love for one another. This book is truly a light in our dark world and invites us to live out the Kingdom of God's imperatives given by our King in John 17. Thank you, Dave, for shining light where we need enlightenment.

Randy Reynolds
Director, Community Renewal

Una perspectiva amplia de la unidad de la iglesia de Jesucristo y sus diferentes aplicaciones. Este libro te lleva a observar diferentes puntos de la unidad que son esenciales y que por ignorancia o por conveniencia los omitimos.

Angel Morfin
Iglesia de JesuCristo Peniel

My amigo Dave Drum is the most qualified man I know to write on John 17 of the Gospel of Jesus Christ. I can say this experientially because as a pastor of a Spanish-speaking church, I watched as Dave built the bridge from where he was to where I was, and then I saw Dave cross the bridge. I'm probably a microorganism somewhere on the toenail of the smallest toe of the left foot of the body. I believe that an eye in the body of Christ saw us, built a bridge, crossed over, and began fellowshipping with us. Thank you again, Dave, for writing this book that shows everybody the art of looking for those in the body that appear to have less dignity than others.

Isaac Martinez
Senior Pastor, Centro Familiar Fuente de Vida

JESUS' SURPRISING STRATEGY

A mandate and a means for
city transformation

David Drum

Adam Colwell's
writeworks

Edited by Adam Colwell
Cover design by Jaime Anaya
Typesetting by Andrew MacKay
Printing by Arizona Lithographers
Distribution by Anchor Distributing
ISBN 978-0-9892057-0-2

Adam Colwell's WriteWorks Publishing
Adam Colwell's WriteWorks LLC, Tucson, AZ
Printed in the United States of America

www.jesussurprisingstrategy.com

Printed with *100% New Wind Energy*

DEDICATION

To my Lord and Savior Jesus Christ, full of grace and truth.
May your name become the most famous name in our city.

ACKNOWLEDGEMENTS

I've had a desire to write for many years, and many people have encouraged me in that regard. Without their encouragement, this project would never have come to completion.

My wonderful wife of 25 years is the person I most admire on this earth. Her grace, her strength, her single-minded devotion to growing in Jesus—and her voice like an angel's—bring light and joy to my life. Thank you, Valerie, for being my soul mate.

My four children, Michael, Amy, Daniel, and Emily, are all amazing and gifted people. I can't imagine life without any of you! Thanks so much for encouraging me to write, and occasionally asking how it's going.

I've always found it a challenge to complete tasks before the absolute last minute. That makes writing a book extremely challenging, because the deadlines are largely self-imposed. Without the unwavering cheerleading, partnership, and encouragement of my editor, partner, and friend Adam Colwell, I doubt this book would have been completed, and I know it wouldn't have been as complete.

My life coach Dennis Watson has helped me set goals and stay disciplined. More importantly, Dennis, you help me be a better follower of Jesus Christ than I would be without you. My friend and colleague Annette Ladd likewise believed in me and encouraged me when I needed it the most.

Dennis Fuqua, the facilitator for all of our prayer summits, also provided some great coaching, editing, and feedback that sharpened much of the language of this book. Thanks, Dennis—your skillful sensitivity to the Holy Spirit's leading in our prayer summits created the fertile ground from which this project grew.

I want to thank all the people who've made up Community of Hope over the last two-plus decades. I was as green as green can be when you first entrusted me to lead, and most of the lessons in this book I learned with and through you. If I started mentioning names, I wouldn't be able to stop, but thanks for truly being a community of hope for me, my family, one another, and our surrounding neighborhoods.

My 4Tucson teammates are a pure joy to work alongside. At the top of the list is our fearless leader and my dear friend, Mark Harris. Your encouragement is constant, and your leadership is remarkable. I continue to learn new things from you every week. The rest of the team makes every day and week so enjoyable: thank you, my fellow domain leaders Brian Goodall, Bernadette Gruber, Francine Rienstra, Paul Parisi, Karen Stewart, RuthAnn Smithrud, Valarie Valencia, Regina Brown, Tony Simms, and Jerry Hermundslie. And thank you, support staff of Micah Lunsford, Dawn, Jessica, Betsy, and Melissa.

Love for one another at a congregational level is very, very sweet, and so I thank Pastor Rick Leis and all our fellow Christ-followers at Connections Vineyard for being such a great new home base for our family.

For many years my two national networks (LCMC and ARC) contained many of my closest pastoral colleagues. I started listing several of you who I admire so deeply, but couldn't figure out when to stop.

I'm so very grateful for a godly heritage, for Christ-followers throughout my extended family, including parents and grandparents.

In taking the position with 4Tucson, I signed up as a missionary to Tucson, complete with the responsibility of raising my own financial and prayer support. To the dozens of prayer and financial partners, it is no empty statement when I say that I literally could not be doing any of this without your support.

I have the best job in the world because I get to follow God around town and take notes. There are so many amazing men and women of God leading congregations throughout Tucson. And likewise there are Christ-followers of remarkable stature and character in churches all over our city. It is such a high privilege to serve God with each of you.

CONTENTS

Section One

The Mandate of Christian Unity

Chapter One

One Passionate Focus

John 17 is an amazing gift from God. Why? It's the most in-depth look we have at Jesus' prayer life, the longest prayer of His anywhere in the Bible. Andrew Murray wrote a book entitled *With Christ in the School of Prayer*. We enroll in that school simply by examining and praying what Jesus prayed.

How we came to have this gift is something of a mystery. Perhaps the gospel writer John was listening in when Jesus prayed it, and the prayer was emblazoned on his mind. Possibly Jesus shared it with the disciples after the resurrection in one of His appearances to them. Or perhaps the Holy Spirit revealed it to John as he was writing his gospel, since bringing to mind the words of Jesus is one of the Spirit's functions (John 14:26). Regardless of how we came to possess it, we have in John 17 the most extensive, developed, thorough prayer of Jesus ever recorded. We can learn what and how Christ prayed and pray right along with Him. If we want to know that our prayers are aligned with Jesus and bless the heart of the Father, one sure way is to pray what Jesus prayed.

All that alone makes it an amazing gift! But the *context* of the prayer in John 17 only adds to its significance. We get to know exactly what was on Jesus' heart and mind as He headed to the cross. John 17 is what the Lord prayed literally hours before He was arrested later that night and crucified the next day. It's possible that Jesus prayed this prayer in the Upper Room, where He celebrated the Passover with the disciples and changed its significance forever (Luke 22). That same evening, Christ showed the depth of His love for them by donning a towel and doing the dirty work that everyone else thought was beneath them (John 13:1-17). The night was made memorable yet again by the new command Jesus gave His disciples, to love one another in the same manner He loved them (John 13:34-35), a recurring theme in His prayer from John 17. Some commentators have suggested that much of John 14-17 could have happened en route to Gethsemane, with Jesus, for instance, teaching about the vine and the branches (John 15) while walking through a vineyard. It's also possible this section of Scripture includes what Jesus actually prayed while in Gethsemane, especially since John was one of those brought along to accompany Him (Matthew 26:37). We're familiar with another Garden of Gethsemane prayer: "Father, if you are willing, take this cup from me; yet not my will, but yours be done." (Luke 22:42) The John 17 prayer likely happened before that one, and vividly details what was on Jesus' mind as He headed toward His ultimate purpose.

I have no idea how many times I read or taught from John 17 in my nearly 21 years as pastor of Community of Hope in Tucson, Arizona. But when our life experiences change, we notice things that had always been there but we never saw before. Buy a new car and you're immediately shocked at how many other people must've just bought that same model, because you see it at every intersection. That's been my experience with changing contexts from pastoring a local congregation to now working with the whole body of Christians in the city. I've noticed things in John 17 that I'd never seen before. As you see them, your perspective is going to change as well.

AN ETERNAL OUTLOOK

At the beginning of the prayer, Jesus focuses on what we might expect him to: eternal life. "Father, the time has come. Glorify your Son, that your Son may glorify you. For you granted him authority over all people that he might give eternal life to all those you have given him. Now this is eternal life: that they may know you, the only true God, and Jesus Christ, whom you have sent." (John 17:1-3) Jesus knew why He came, and He knew that the cross was the gateway to eternal life. He's focused on His purpose.

"Father, the time has come..." This is crunch time. Coaches teach their team many things during practice, but when it's crunch time, they narrow it down to the one most important thing they want the team to accomplish. In the locker room right before the game, or during a time-out when the clock is in the waning minutes: those are the times to laser focus only on what matters most. Jesus left heaven so that we might experience heaven. The cross is what opens up that possibility. It's not the least bit surprising that perhaps the clearest definition of eternal life in the Bible is found in the beginning of this prayer: "Now this is eternal life: that they may know you, the only true God, and Jesus Christ, whom you have sent."

Earlier that evening, Jesus had explained to them that He was the way, the truth, and the life, and that nobody comes to the Father except through Him (John 14:6). So Jesus is praying some of the same things He taught just hours before.

> **How often does the person praying deliberately tell us what he's not praying?**

In the verses that follow, Jesus explains that He's completing the work He left heaven to do (v. 4), and He asks that He might be restored to the glory that He left behind when leaving heaven for earth (v. 5). Eternal life isn't just a theory or a principle; it's an actual gift purchased at high cost for people. Through Jesus, eternal life is available for all people, and for specific people like you and me. So He starts praying specifically for those closest to Him who "knew with certainty that I came from you [the Father], and believe that you sent me." (v. 8)

STRATEGY REVEALED

John 17:9 makes this prayer totally unique. How many prayers come to mind in the Bible where the person praying tells us what they *aren't* praying? This is the only one I've found. Jesus is praying for His disciples and He says, "I pray for them. I am not praying for the world, but for those you have given me, for they are yours." Christ points out to the Father that He's not praying for the whole world.

Does Jesus care about the entire world? Absolutely. John 3:16 has been called "the Gospel in a nutshell," and has so captured the attention of Christians that it can be found in amazing places: behind the goal posts at football games, on the bottoms of Forever 21 shopping bags, and printed on soft drink cups from In-N-Out Burger stores. "For God so loved the world that he gave his one and only Son…" Jesus isn't arguing with the Father here like a rebellious teenager: "Well, *you* may love the whole world, but *I* sure don't." Not at all! Jesus and the Father are perfectly aligned. As Charles Spurgeon writes in *Morning by Morning*, "In deeds of grace none of the Persons of the Trinity act apart from the rest. They are as united in their deeds as in their essence." So why would Jesus declare that He's not going to pray for the whole world He came to save?

I believe this is a strategic statement—and if we really take it seriously, one that will dramatically change our perspectives and priorities. When time and resources are limited, decisions have to be made. Jesus strategically decided to focus His prayers on those who are already His followers. He did this because He knew the way to reach the world starts with those He personally discipled. Think about that. Jesus is placing the rest of the world in the hands of those He reached. That's amazing. It's not an indication of favoritism. It's a statement of strategy.

"One" passionate focus

What does He pray for His disciples? "Holy Father, protect them by the power of your name—the name you gave me—so that they may be one as we are one." (John 17:11) Jesus prays that His followers would be one: unified not at some trite level, but rather in the same way the Father and Son are unified. Christ repeatedly prays that same request (vs. 21, 22 and 23). Clearly, this is His passionate focus in this prayer. What has been growing in depth and significance to me is how strategic Jesus is about this prayer and how much of the rest of the prayer qualifies and explains and develops this one focus of unity. We quickly discover Jesus doesn't leave the definition of unity to whichever way the wind might happen to be blowing. He's crystal clear about what unity is, and His conclusions are extraordinary.

1. It's not a *private* unity

One of the first misconceptions about Christian unity shows up in verse 15. "My prayer is not that you take them out of the world but that you protect them from the evil one." As we saw before, when Jesus makes a point of telling us what He's *not* praying, we should pay extra attention. Jesus will not pray that Christians be removed from the world. In fact, He prays and teaches the opposite: Christians are to be salt and light for the world (Matthew 5:13-14), influencing and shaping the world in which we live.

For far too long, local churches have functioned like monasteries, isolated from the neighborhoods where they're placed, sometimes quite intentionally. "Jesus taught us to love one another," we might say, as if that gives us not only permission but blessing to withdraw from our culture. What we forget is "love one another" isn't the end, it's the means to an end: "By this all people will know that you are my disciples, if you have love for one another." (John 13:35 ESV) How can "all people" know anything at all about us if there's never any interaction between "us" and "them?"

Community of Hope was situated on a street with a fair amount of traffic. Thousands of cars would pass by every day. We would put up signs advertising various things happening inside the walls, but rarely would anyone check it out just because of those

> For too long, churches have functioned like monasteries.

signs. I'm convinced people drive by churches every day without ever giving a thought to walking in, not because they're opposed to the church, but more because the church is irrelevant to them. Stopping in never crosses their minds. It's like driving by a foreign country, minus the excitement and intrigue that comes from visiting one.

It's becoming far easier to meet people who don't know any Christians (or don't know they do because the Christians have never revealed their primary allegiance). It's likewise altogether common for Christians to say they don't really know any non-believers. All their relationship capital has been invested in other Christians. Community of Hope grew steadily its first 15 years, but its menu of programs grew even faster. I remember teaching a class about sharing Christ in the relationships we already have with non-Christians. Several people told me they didn't know any non-Christians. They were spending several nights a week in our church building, but had no time to invest in the lives of those outside the church walls.

This is not the unity that Jesus was praying for. He wasn't praying that we'd become a holy huddle, a private club, a Bible bunch that comes across as exclusive. The vast majority of churches don't want to be perceived this way: every church I know would claim to believe in the Great Commission (Matthew 28:16-20). But we come across as exclusive because we aren't actively doing anything to build relationships with the world at our doorsteps. Our situation is quite similar to that of the Israelites in exile in Babylon. We're living in an increasingly foreign land, with values at odds with those revealed in the Bible. It must have been tempting for the Israelites to develop an internal unity mindset: "Our job here in this foreign land is simply to survive, to preserve our identity as the faithful remnant, to hold out until better days arrive." Yet God addressed that temptation in the strongest way possible. "Seek the peace and prosperity of the city to which I have carried you into exile. Pray to the LORD for it, because if it prospers, you too will prosper." (Jeremiah 29:7)

If that can be true for Babylon, it certainly applies to the cities in which we live. Jesus directly tells us that the unity He's praying for among His followers will not be a private unity.

2. It's not a *watered-down* unity

So was Rodney King right? His famous line from the 1991 Los Angeles riots was, "Can we all get along?" King reflected the prevailing opinion of modern society: it doesn't matter what people believe as long as they're sincere. Really? Beliefs sincerely held by terrorists are the same as beliefs sincerely held by Boy Scouts? It's astounding anyone could be so naïve as to think that the way to achieve unity is to throw out all reference to absolute truth, and yet we hear it all the time. Tolerance is society's god; that is, unless you happen to not bow down to it. Don't expect much tolerance for that.

Jesus is Lord in every age. He addressed our twenty-first century challenges way back in first century Palestine. "Sanctify them by the truth; your word is truth." (John 17:17) Christ prays that His followers would be sanctified, not that they

Truth and unity are on the same team.

would learn to blend in. What is most instrumental in that sanctification process? The Word of God. The truth of God's Word is what ultimately leads to a unity that lasts.

If unity and truth are somehow seen as being in opposition to one another, both unity and truth are lost. A unity that has no reference to truth is merely a surface-level commitment to be nice. At the first sign of conflict, the relationship ceases to grow and likely retreats significantly. Similarly, a pursuit of truth that has unity as a casualty is probably less about truth and more about pride and arrogance. The author of the John 17 prayer is the same Jesus who earlier that evening taught His unique relationship to the Father (John 14:6), and earlier in the same prayer defined eternal life as knowing Jesus, sent by the Father. We won't be answering Jesus' prayer if we seek a unity that bypasses Him.

Truth and unity are on the same team. They're in the same prayer, and Jesus is the one praying it. We must never forget that.

3. IT'S NOT A *FIRST-CENTURY ONLY* UNITY

Finally, Jesus' strategic emphasis to focus on the unity of His followers was not limited to the time He was on earth. It's His strategy in every age. "My prayer is not for them alone. I pray also for those who will believe in me through their message, that all of them may be one, Father, just as you are in me and I am in you." (John 17:20-21) Whenever I teach this point, I always ask the audience, "Who is Jesus praying for here?" Every audience gets it: He's praying for us. We're the ones who believe in Jesus through the good news passed down by the disciples. As Emmanuel, God in the flesh, He actually had the capacity to pray for people by name who were not yet born. Jesus prays in that moment that the believers in your city, this very day, would be unified in the same way that Father and Son are unified as one.

Historians from the first few centuries A.D.—Tertullian, Justin Martyr, Clement—record that Jesus' strategy actually worked. They reported that the pagan and cruel Roman emperors who took delight in discovering new and sadistic ways to kill Christians also were awestruck by these Christians: "See how they love one another," they're quoted as saying. The unity that captured their attention was not merely a private internal unity. When plagues and epidemics spread through the land and everyone's inclination was to head to the hills, Christians stayed behind and cared for the sick and dying, often at the expense of their own lives. A strong case can be made that what ultimately brought down the Roman Empire was not a stronger military presence belonging to someone else, but Christians whose love for one another actually functioned like salt and light in the world. As author and teacher John Ortberg points out, today we name children after the disciples (Matthew, Peter, Philip, and John) while we name our dogs after Roman emperors (Caesar and Brutus). "See how they love one another" indicates what caused that stunning reversal.

How the first century believers loved one another—and all those around them—made a profound, history-altering difference. What was true in the years after Jesus' birth, death, resurrection and ascension can be equally true in our day. Jesus directly and specifically prayed that it would be. He is giving us His strategy for changing our world.

UNITY'S ULTIMATE PURPOSE

Now we come full circle. Christian unity is not an end, but a means to an end. "May they be brought to complete unity to let the world know that you sent me and have loved them even as you have loved me." (John 17:23) There's a powerful "so that" at the end of Jesus' thought. He prays for complete unity among Christian believers—so that the world may know His true identity and undying love. Unity is not an internal thing; it's supposed to be external, visible to a watching world. We are the body of Christ together in our city.

The eternal life that Jesus came to secure at the cost of His life is strategically packaged in visible, substantive Christian unity. What kind of unity would capture the world's attention so compellingly they would be clamoring at our doors trying to discover its source?

- A unity that can only be explained by Jesus Christ.

- A unity that binds together those with nothing else in common but Him.

- A unity and love for one another that not only transcends racial and denominational differences, but comes to appreciate the unique perspectives each brings to the table.

- A unity that takes the lead in addressing and solving some of the world's most vexing problems.

- A unity that brings Christians together not only in the confines of the congregation, but everywhere else where people spend time—in media, government, business, education, sports, the environment, health care, and so on—arriving at solutions only God can ultimately provide.

Yes, John 17 is an incredible gift. When you look around at your city and its legion of problems, it's easy to feel overwhelmed and incapacitated. I love my city of Tucson, Arizona. I was born there and anticipate dying there, but Tucson is in serious need of transformation. How do I start addressing that need? By focusing on what Jesus focused on when at the apex of intensity and purpose. Jesus had eternity on His mind, but strategically chose to focus His love for the world by praying for His followers. He prayed His followers would be visibly united in the same way that the Father and Son are united. He prayed that Christian unity would spill out of the doors of churches and into the world He created and came to redeem. He prayed that this unity would be shaped by the Word of God and that believers would be sanctified by

11

His truth. He prayed that as a result of what the world saw in His followers, knowledge of God's identity and love would grow.

Of course, Christian unity had its enemies then as it does now. Yet one of its greatest foes not only became a champion for unity, he took Jesus' John 17 prayer and gave it an added relevance that helped birth the Christian Church, spread the gospel, and provide an analogy for transformation that you can use today, right now, to change your city. But be warned. It'll change you, too!

Chapter Two

Paul's Citywide Analogy

Jesus' disciples had a lot of time after the resurrection to reflect on what had happened and what it all meant. Their whole world had been flipped upside down not once, but twice; first, when the One they'd come to trust as the hope of the world was cruelly tortured and executed like a common criminal; and second, when Jesus upended death itself, defeating the last enemy standing.

Every so often, Jesus would "appear"—showing up unexpectedly and seemingly out of nowhere. It seems that the disciples did what I would have done—hang out at the last place I saw Him, hoping it becomes a pattern. So back to the Upper Room they went, and not only did Jesus reveal a penchant for the place, but possibly the day and time as well. Sunday evening in the Upper Room was the place to be for two weeks in a row. Christ transformed that place and that day completely by His presence.

When that didn't work any longer and the disciples were unsure what to do next, they reverted back to old habits. Peter announced, "I'm going fishing," and many of the rest joined him, returning to their "before Christ" professions as fishermen. Of course, when Jesus appeared to them at the lake, too, He had the effect of immediately transforming their work environment. That was not accidental, nor is it irrelevant. Christ isn't just interested in the "holy" (or, quite literally, "set apart") places like the Upper Room; He's interested in people, wherever they are. The disciples would eventually learn His purpose is to transform every environment, not just the "sacred" ones.

After Jesus ascended into heaven, the disciples were really left dangling. He wasn't coming back, at least not anytime soon: He told them so directly. He commissioned them to go make disciples of a waiting, watching world. But not yet—He didn't want them messing things up in their own strength, so He told them to wait in Jerusalem until the Holy Spirit came. But when would that be? How would they know when it happened?

What did the disciples do while they waited an undetermined amount of time for an unclear event to occur? They unified—through prayer. "They all joined together constantly in prayer, along with the women and Mary the mother of Jesus, and with his brothers." (Acts 1:14) For 10 days, as it turned out, they did the hard work of unifying. Unity doesn't stop at home, but it sure needs to *start* there.

Unifying the first Church

When you think about how much unifying work they had to do, it's amazing it only took a few days: "When the day of Pentecost came, they were all together in one place." (Acts 2:1) The beginning of Acts 2 is far more than a statement of geography. It's a declaration that the divisions that could have torn them apart had been adequately dealt with through prayer. Had they spent the week and a half merely talking with one another and not in an atmosphere of prayer, I'm certain 10 days would have been wholly inadequate. Ten years likely wouldn't have done it. True prayer requires humility, an absolutely necessary ingredient for visible unity, and praying with one another is one of the most effective ways to unify, whether the pray-ers constitute a couple in a marriage or all the Christians in a city.

What all had to be worked out among the disciples? Mere weeks earlier, Peter had boldly announced that even if all the rest of these schmucks turned their backs on Jesus, *he* never would (Luke 22:33). I'm sure that set well with everyone. Meanwhile, James and John asked Jesus for the best seats in the house—and got their mother in on the plot, too (Mark 10:35-45; Matthew 20:20-28). Who knows whether the argument that broke out as a result was because the rest of the disciples were angry at the brothers' audacity, or jealous they hadn't thought of it first? When it became apparent that Jesus' kingdom wasn't going to overthrow the Romans, the fact that one of them (Matthew) was a Roman employee probably resurfaced. Thomas ditched them right after the resurrection and ended up getting rewarded with a command performance (John 20:24-29). Someone should have noticed Judas skimming off the treasury, and there would have been ample opportunity to point fingers at one another (John 12:1-6).

> **Somehow Paul learned about Jesus' surprising strategy.**

That doesn't even cover all the challenges within the group! Suppose there could have been any friction with any of the women? Or the fact that Jesus picked out John to personally care for his mother? How about perhaps the biggest unity challenge of all, tossed in almost as a footnote to Acts 1:14? Jesus' *brothers* had joined the crowd, the same ones who were totally absent throughout His ministry, convinced Jesus was out of His mind or worse. Yet who would end up becoming the identified leader of the Christians within a few years? James, Jesus' brother. That doesn't happen without an absolutely intentional focus on doing the necessary work to unify.

PAUL PICKS UP THE BATON

Arguably the key human figure in the whole New Testament missed all of this. The apostle Paul was on the other side of this river of unity. He probably was in the crowd at Pentecost in Acts 2, seeing the disciples filled with the Spirit and hearing Peter's blistering sermon. If Paul (also known as Saul) was there that day, he wasn't one of the 3,000 to repent and be baptized. By the end of Acts 7, Paul is Christian enemy number one, and only the power of God was capable of knocking him off his high horse.

At some point after Paul switched sides and became a Christ-follower (recorded in Acts 9), I believe he learned about Jesus' John 17 prayer.

Whether the disciples told him, the Holy Spirit told him, or he just saw it lived out among a highly unlikely group of soul mates, somehow Paul learned about Jesus' surprising strategy, the one that had warranted the sole focus of His prayer life on the way to the cross.

As powerful as Jesus' John 17 prayer is, it doesn't give a lot of specifics about what this unity looks like in everyday life. That's why God used the apostle Paul to flesh out the prayer of His Son. Paul took Jesus' prayer for unity in John 17 and developed it into an extended analogy for the Church in 1 Corinthians 12. The Church, Paul wrote, is like a human body with many parts. The parts aren't identical in appearance or in function—and it's by design! Yet when all the parts are properly connected to the head, Jesus Christ, they will also be connected to one another. When one part suffers, the whole body suffers. When one part rejoices, the whole body rejoices.

THE STARTING POINT WHEN YOU THINK "CHURCH" IS...

So who was Paul writing to when he wrote 1 Corinthians 12? It's not who you think, because he wasn't writing to a single congregation known as the Corinthians. He was writing to a *collection* of congregations in the city of Corinth. He was writing to the city.

Such an assertion is particularly counterintuitive in the United States where individualism is one of the strongest worldviews, filtering out what's assumed in most of the rest of the world. Americans tend to read most New Testament sentences as if they're written to them as individuals, but in most cases the "you" is plural. People in many other nations understand this intuitively: they think collectively rather than individually. Yet expanding our naturally individualistic tendencies to include a whole congregation is not a sign of enlightenment—it's just further indication of our entrapment. We almost always view congregations from an individual perspective, but that concept is foreign to the New Testament. "Church" in the New Testament is all the Christians in a city.

CITY CHURCH IN REVELATION

The book of Revelation is written as a letter to seven churches in the province of Asia (Revelation 1:4). What do all those seven churches have in common? They were not just local congregations. Ephesus, Smyrna, Pergamum, Thyatira, Sardis, Philadelphia, and Laodicea were all cities. These weren't towns along the missionary byway, either. Ephesus, the first church mentioned in the list, had a population of 250,000, making it the second largest city in the world at the time. Parallels today would be Seoul, South Korea and Mexico City, Mexico. In addition, remember that Christians didn't have their own church buildings until the fourth century. They met in houses, so the size of a congregation was limited to the size of the house. Ephesus, therefore, would've had many churches, yet John wrote Revelation to the city church there and the other six locations.

CITY CHURCH IN ROMANS

Romans is rare among the New Testament epistles written by Paul because it was written to a church that he hadn't personally established and had never visited before. At the close of the letter, Paul therefore went to great lengths in establishing points of contact. Just reading through Romans 16, we get a great peak into first century church demographics.

16:1 – the church in Cenchrea (a port near Corinth; Corinth's population was 200,000).

16:4 – "all the churches of the Gentiles."

16:5 – "the church that meets at (Priscilla's and Aquila's) house."

16:10, 11– the households of Aristobulus and Narcissus, both probably the basis of churches.

16:16 – "All the churches of Christ send greetings."

16:17   –   "I urge you, brothers to watch out for those who cause divisions…"

City church in Acts

Acts 1:8 is the author Luke's version of the Great Commission in Matthew 28. "But you will receive power when the Holy Spirit comes on you; and you will be my witnesses in Jerusalem, and in all Judea and Samaria, and to the ends of the earth." Where does the commission start? In Jerusalem: the city. From an individualistic standpoint, we would expect our witnessing to start within our personal "spheres of influence." While I'm not arguing against the power of friendship evangelism, it's noteworthy that Acts 1:8 doesn't start from an individualistic perspective. It's a city church, witnessing to all the people in a city. The "you," once again, is plural. Even Jesus' evangelism analogy of fishing in Matthew 4:19 ("From now on, you will fish for people.") isn't the individual experience of taking the tackle box and fishing pole out to the lake. They fished with nets and it was a group effort.

House churches were the norm and there were many of them.

City church in 1 Corinthians

While the books of Revelation, Acts, and Romans all paint a picture of the city as the basic building block of the church, it's even easier to see in 1 Corinthians, the letter in which Paul's analogy of the church as a body receives its most complete development. At the end of the book, we find a list of greetings similar (though less extensive) to the end of Romans: "The churches in the province of Asia send you greetings. Aquila and Priscilla greet you warmly in the Lord, and so does the church that meets at their house." (1 Corinthians 16:19) House churches were the norm and there were many of them.

A lack of unity within the city church was one of the main reasons Paul wrote to the Corinthians. "I appeal to you, brothers, in the name of our Lord Jesus Christ, that all of you agree with one another so that there may be no divisions among you and that you may be perfectly united in mind and thought." (1 Corinthians 1:10) Read that passage twice: first thinking of a single, local congregation, then again in the mindset of all the congregations in the area like Paul intended. Notice the difference in perspective? He continues: "My brothers, some from Chloe's household [one congregation in Corinth] have informed me that there are quarrels among you [the various congregations in the city]. What I mean is this: One of you says, 'I follow Paul'; another, 'I follow Apollos'; another, 'I follow Cephas'; still another, 'I follow Christ.'" (1 Corinthians 1:11-12) Ecclesiastes 1:9 says, "There is nothing new under the sun," and that's certainly true here. To contemporize the passage, "One congregation says, 'We follow Luther;' another, "We follow Calvin;' still another, 'We follow Wimber;' and another, 'We don't believe in all that denominational stuff. We just follow Christ!'" It could be rewritten any number of ways and hold true. "We're part of the Hispanic pastors association" and list various ethnic groups that make up the city; or "We're purpose driven and follow Warren," while others might teach against such perspectives. "We're suburban," "We're urban," "We're rural," "We're traditional," "We're contemporary," "We're emerging." There is practically no end to the identifiable divisions.

> We have churches on different corners, like McDonalds and Burger King, competing for market share.

Earlier in the chapter Paul commends them for being "enriched in every way" and "not lacking any spiritual gift." Again, these assertions are true of the whole church in Corinth collectively but not of any individual house church. Paul is writing to the city church—the letter is addressed "to the church [singular] in Corinth," meaning every individual congregation in Corinth was to see themselves as part of the one Christian church in the city.

Paul later adds: "Brothers, I could not address you as spiritual, but as worldly—mere infants in Christ. I gave you milk, not solid food, for you were not yet ready for it. Indeed, you are still not ready. You are still worldly. For since there is jealousy and quarreling among you, are you not worldly?" (1 Corinthians 3:1-3) The similarity to churches today is staggering! We have churches on different corners, like McDonalds and Burger King, competing for market share. Plus, these churches are contaminated with jealousy (over another church's size, facilities, musicians, youth program, staff or money, etc.) and quarreling (over language, worship style, theological preference, expressiveness or the lack of it, etc.). Churches in America are just like those in Corinth. It's profoundly sad. Yet this is where Paul's citywide analogy, and his development of Jesus' surprising strategy from John 17, becomes such a practical picture for today's city church.

THE BODY OF CHRIST

"Just as a body, though one, has many parts, but all its many parts form one body, so it is with Christ. For we were all baptized by one Spirit so as to form one body—whether Jews or Gentiles, slave or free—and we were all given the one Spirit to drink. Even so the body is not made up of one part but of many.

"Now if the foot should say, 'Because I am not a hand, I do not belong to the body,' it would not for that reason stop being part of the body. And if the ear should say, 'Because I am not an eye, I do not belong to the body,' it would not for that reason stop being part of the body. If the whole body were an eye, where would the sense of hearing be? If the whole body were an ear, where would the sense of smell be? But in fact God has placed the parts in the body, every one of them, just as he wanted them to be. If they were all one part, where would the body be? As it is, there are many parts, but one body.

"The eye cannot say to the hand, 'I don't need you!' And the head cannot say to the feet, 'I don't need you!' On the contrary, those parts of the body that seem to be weaker are indispensable, and the parts that we think are less honorable we treat with special honor. And the parts that are unpresentable are treated with special modesty, while our presentable parts need no special treatment. But God has put the body together, giving greater honor to the parts that lacked it, so that there should be no division in the body, but that its parts should have equal concern for each other. If one part suffers, every part suffers with it; if one part is honored, every part rejoices with it. Now you are the body of Christ, and each one of you is a part of it." (1 Corinthians 12:12-27 NIV 2011)

Most of the times I've read that passage, I've thought of it with respect to the local congregation. There can be both feelings of inferiority that divide the body ("Why does he always get to lead?" or "I could never sing like that.") as well as feelings of superiority ("The kids of this generation just can't seem to show any respect," or "Those old people just don't get it."). People who serve in the kitchen ministries need to know they're just as vital to the body as Sunday school teachers. Those applications certainly work and are faithful to the text.

But I'm convinced that the primary application Paul had in mind in his passage was the city church, even way back in his day. God has designed the various congregations in a geographic area to have different characteristics and varying strengths. No one part of the body will be good at everything. Sociologists have helped us understand that everyone approaches every situation from a vantage point based on their experience. Bias is unavoidable; it's impossible to approach a situation with complete objectivity. The same is true within the Christian Church. Our theological traditions are a gift, but they also function as a lens and a worldview, causing us to filter out foreign objects. We all have blind spots. Nobody has the complete picture.

Small congregations can develop an inferiority complex. Large congregations can develop an island mentality, where they act as if they don't need the smaller congregations, even if they would never say so (though, sadly, sometimes they do). Poor congregations with rundown facilities can see themselves as incapable of making much of a difference, when in fact some poor people who are feeling rundown themselves feel right at home there. Rich congregations with hotel quality facilities can be accused of having their priorities all messed up, when in fact some rich people won't even enter to hear about Jesus unless the facilities are top notch.

Yet even if we were successful in fully uniting the various expressions of the church within a city, we'd still have only addressed one aspect of Paul's multilayered, citywide analogy. If we understand "church" as being the facilities, the worship service, or programs the local congregation offers, that's only one small piece of the puzzle. Outside of staff, most Christians spend no more than a few hours a week at "church;" rather, they spend the vast majority of their time in business, education, government, or any of a wide variety of other environments and spheres of influence. When congregations pull people out of these places in order to get them to serve solely *in* the "church," they're doing the opposite of what Jesus taught. The church becomes a "desalination plant," removing salt from the world, as Reggie McNeal states in his book *Missional Renaissance: Changing the Scorecard for the Church*. Paul envisions Christians being *in* every aspect of society, working together as a body, unified under the sovereign leadership of the head of that body, Jesus Christ. Paul wants us to learn the same lesson the fisherman disciples learned: Jesus' presence made them better fishermen, too.

A common refrain in the Old Testament is that God is a jealous God. He's not interested in sharing His glory with anyone. "I am the LORD; that is my name! I will not give my glory to anyone else." (Isaiah 42:8 NLT) I'm convinced God will not *allow* one subgroup of the Christian church—be it a congregation, denomination, network, or ethnic branch—to have total lasting transformational success in a city, because what would happen if one of those subgroups was successful? All credit would be given to that subgroup. That would be as silly as singing, "All hail the big toes." Jesus is the head of the body, so He alone deserves the accolades and praise. Only a visibly unified body, functioning as a unit for the sake of the city, will cause the attention of the city to turn to the Lord in charge. "Let your light so shine before men, that they may see your good deeds and praise your Father in heaven." (Matthew 5:16) The "your" is plural in that verse, and it primarily applies to the Christians in a city.

As a principle, I've chosen to use "congregation" throughout these chapters to refer to a local gathering of believers; "church" to refer to all the believers in a city; and "Church" (with a capital C) to refer to something larger than a city—either an entire denomination or usually the whole Christian Church. There are instances where church refers to a local congregation: when the language would be too wordy or so different from standard usage as to be clumsy or awkward. And in a few instances I've put quotation marks around church to indicate usage of the word that clearly contradicts its biblical meaning.

The only way God gets the glory is if we're being church *together*. The only way for unity of that magnitude to exist and function is when you decide to fully invest yourself in your city and, more specifically, what Jesus wants to accomplish in your city.

Chapter Three

Investing or Cheering?

Jesus can be your stockbroker—if you'll let Him. You can invest in the things that Jesus invests in, and it's unlikely you'll outdo His investment strategy.

Hopefully you're convinced: unity in the body of Christ is not optional. If unity isn't a priority for us, we're out of line with the prayers of God's only Son. And the unity that Jesus prayed for and the New Testament describes is not just an internal unity within a local congregation. It's a visible, citywide unity, profound enough to catch the attention of a watching world.

I don't know anyone in the Christian community who thinks unity is a bad idea. Some leaders badmouth other leaders consistently, and find a heresy behind almost every bush: bushes planted on somebody else's property, of course. But I've never heard even notoriously poor team players go so far as to argue against John 17.

I know some who argue from a theological perspective that the invisible Church (all Christians in every time and place) is already united. The one, holy, catholic (meaning universal, not just Roman Catholic) and apostolic Church, as the Nicene Creed puts it, is and always will be one. I don't argue against that—theologically. But I don't notice any disclaimers in John 17 or 1 Corinthians 12 saying as long as we understand ourselves to be unified theologically or spiritually we don't have to pay any attention to the concept practically. The world doesn't draw its conclusions about the church from theology textbooks. Opinions are formed by the actual interaction, or lack of it, with the church next door—and that congregation's interaction, or lack of it, with other congregations in the city.

In some settings, unity is a phrase that implies structural togetherness; for example, denominations merging and coming under one organizational umbrella. I spent my seminary training and first 11 years as a pastor in a denomination that paid way too much attention to structural unity. Why should it take several years and several hundred thousand dollars for academic theologians to hammer out full communion agreements in order to produce altar and pulpit fellowship (meaning that pastors can preach in one another's pulpits, and people can commune at one another's tables)? Even if such a level of agreement is achieved between denominational headquarters, it still doesn't even approach the unity described in the New Testament. Neither John 17 nor 1 Corinthians 12 need to be that complicated. We don't need a treatise on all the nuances of who "one another" really is; we simply need to learn to love one another on a completely practical level. The visible unity prayed for by Jesus and built upon by Paul has almost nothing to do with organizational structure. It has everything to do with people on the street *seeing* it. When they experience the body of Christ in action in their city, unity is what they see.

Visible unity has almost nothing to do with organizational structure.

INVESTMENT INCENTIVES

My desire for Christian unity is deeply personal. When I was growing up, church unity (or the lack of it) showed up at my dinner table. My dad was raised Evangelical United Brethren, which eventually merged with the United Methodist Church but really feels more Baptist than anything. My mom grew up Lutheran. When the two of them got married, the Lutherans won out—for awhile. After a couple of bad experiences with Lutheran churches, my dad went back to his Baptist roots and then some related offshoots in the Nazarene Church. At one point in high school, my dad was on staff as a musician in a Baptist church while my mom was on staff as a Christian education director in a Lutheran church. I care quite a bit about Christians of different flavors learning to love one another! But even personal incentives such as those I grew up with don't necessarily mean that fans of Christian unity become investors in Christian unity.

I graduated from Lutheran seminary and began pastoring Community of Hope Lutheran Church in Tucson in fall 1990. I came in knowing I wanted to be a team player. Somehow that value is part of my DNA. It's related to the spiritual gift of pastoring, which surfaced in my formative years long before I ever considered becoming a pastor. Nobody had to convince me being a team player was a good thing. I've never understood a "lone ranger" mentality.

Here, though, was the problem: my definition of team was way too small. My first understanding of the concept was my local congregation. I knew it was critically important that the congregation I led function as a unified team, and it took up most of my time, energy, and prayers. While it's certainly appropriate that pastors of local churches prioritize tending to their local congregation, nobody could look at my life then and say I was investing in the *city* in any substantial way. I had reduced the Kingdom of God to the local congregation, the one with the sign out front that had my name on it.

Yet even then I knew instinctively that the Church was bigger than my local congregation, so I did allow a little bit of time to build relationships with other pastors. Here's where my myopic vision in those days makes me want to cry today. My understanding of being a team player from a citywide context meant meeting with other Lutheran pastors. Even that is overstated. I made time to meet only with other Lutheran pastors who were the *same kind of Lutheran* I was.

Roy became a member of our congregation shortly after I became pastor. I later learned he functioned informally as something of an elder in the city church. He'd been raised Lutheran but had a view of church bigger than just one denomination. He invited me to come to a couple monthly citywide gatherings of pastors: one was the Tucson Association of Evangelicals; the other was Coalition of Prayer Network. I told him that sounded like a great idea. I was a fan. I'd be sure to come if I had time. Yet each month would roll around and I'd find something more important to do. I probably made one of those bigger-than-just-Lutherans pastors' gatherings about once or twice a year. This went on for over five years. Even when I would come, I usually arrived late and left early. I was so very busy tending to my own little kingdom.

Finally God caught my attention. Here's what He told me: "Dave, what could you possibly be doing that's so important that you can't invest an hour or two a month in connecting to the city church?" I had no answer for Him. That was the beginning of a big year of repentance for me. From that day forward, those meetings became priorities. I stopped gauging my attendance on my interest in the topic or my knowledge of the speaker. Rather, it became part of my responsibility as a pastor in the city, something that became a fixture in my schedule that everything else had to fit around. I attended those gatherings to build relationships with other pastors, and if my mind got tickled by the topic, that was a bonus.

Jesus didn't pray for fans of Christian unity, cheering it on from the safe distance of your seat. He prayed for *investors* in it—people who would get in the game. Paul wasn't describing the Church as a theory. He was painting a picture of the Church in reality. The New Testament envisions real-life Christians in real-time cities, engaged and actually functioning as one unified body under the headship of Jesus Christ. And since we have an enemy who loves to steal, kill, and destroy (John 10:10), it's guaranteed that if unity isn't a practical priority we're actively involved in pursuing, it won't be achieved.

> If unity isn't a practical priority we're actively involved in pursuing, it won't be achieved.

What Investing Looks Like

In the physical realm, when a body part gets disconnected from the rest of the body, it's called amputation. There's nothing pretty about amputation. Nobody celebrates it.

Sadly, amputation is the norm in the body of Christ. It's seen as a regular occurrence and, in some cases, required. The more "enlightened" member of the Christian Church might have branched out to associate with their theological neighbors, but it's exceedingly rare to find many who are comfortable with and appreciative of the whole wide range of gifts and perspectives that God designed for His body. There are parts of the body that have never even communicated with other parts. There are some denominations where their pastors actually get in trouble if they start hanging out with other parts of the Church body. I remember the first time Community of Hope hosted a city-wide gathering of Tucson Association of Evangelicals. I shared at the start of the meeting a little bit of what we believe as Lutherans. I knew there were some in attendance who thought Lutherans elevated Martin Luther like Mormons elevate Joseph Smith. I actually had two pastors of non-denominational churches come up to me afterwards and thank me because, until that meeting, they hadn't realized Lutherans could be Christians.

Only by investing in Christian unity will we consistently achieve it to any degree. If those two pastors hadn't invested that hour and a half by coming to foreign territory—a Lutheran church—they still would have been the non-denominational "eye" of the body of Christ saying to the denominational "hand" of the body, "I don't need you." (1 Corinthians 12:21)

Reciting an ecumenical creed (the Apostles' Creed or Nicene Creed—see next page) during worship doesn't make a person ecumenical. There's nothing wrong with doing so; we did it at Community of Hope's traditional service every Sunday for the two decades I was their pastor. But until we actually get to know others who have never heard of the Nicene Creed, but happen to believe everything in it, we're just talking into the wind. Incidentally, the word ecumenical is a Greek word that literally

29

The Nicene Creed

We believe in one God, the Father, the Almighty, maker of heaven and earth, of all that is, seen and unseen.

We believe in one Lord, Jesus Christ, the only Son of God, eternally begotten of the Father, God from God, Light from Light, true God from true God, begotten, not made, of one Being with the Father; through Him all things were made. For us and for our salvation He came down from heaven, was incarnate of the Holy Spirit and the virgin Mary and became truly human. For our sake He was crucified under Pontius Pilate; He suffered death and was buried. On the third day He rose again in accordance with the Scriptures; He ascended into heaven and is seated at the right hand of the Father. He will come again in glory to judge the living and the dead, and His kingdom will have no end.

We believe in the Holy Spirit, the Lord, the giver of life, who proceeds from the Father and the Son, who with the Father and the Son is worshiped and glorified, who has spoken through the prophets. We believe in one holy catholic and apostolic Church. We acknowledge one Baptism for the forgiveness of sins. We look for the resurrection of the dead, and the life of the world to come. Amen.

means "one house" (*oikos* = house; *menos* = one). Ecumenical, then, refers to different rooms within the same house, not different houses altogether. The term "interfaith" refers to different houses. The ecumenical movement within Christianity refers to relationships between different Christian denominations which all recognize one Lord and Savior, Jesus Christ. Interfaith refers to relationships between different religions. My passion refers to ecumenism among Christians. That's what Jesus was praying for and Paul was describing.

I've gained much from ecumenism. I learned a love for the written Word of God from Lutherans. I learned the importance of evangelism from Baptists. I learned to lean into the work of the Holy Spirit from Charismatics. I learned about the spiritual gift of healing from the Vineyard. I learned about discipleship from the Navigators. Richard Foster and some Catholic friends impacted me in regards to prayer. It was a Presbyterian (Eugene Peterson) who helped shape much of my pastoral identity. I learned about reaching into the community from some of my Hispanic and African American sisters and brothers. Global Christians have shown me what true commitment looks like.

The goal of Christian unity isn't to end all denominations, and I'm not really convinced that having a plethora of denominations is necessarily even a problem. If we take Paul's analogy of the church seriously, God's *desire and design* is different body parts with different perspectives, emphases, and functions. Whether those differences get denominational labels or not isn't the point, and like-minded people grouping together is inevitable. In our human bodies, fingers and toes tend to hang out next to other fingers and toes rather than being randomly placed throughout the body. The point is whether or not we'll take Jesus' prayer seriously and employ His strategy in living out a citywide church.

MY CITY'S GAME CHANGER

In 2009, about two dozen pastors from a wide variety of congregations, denominations, and races in Tucson spent Monday evening through Thursday noon together praying for one another and for the city at a pastor's prayer summit. The first time I heard about it, my reaction was, "Four days? Are you kidding? There's no way I can invest four days in something like that." I'd become pretty proud of myself for investing significant chunks of time in building relationships among pastors and denominations, but four days seemed over the top. I'd never spent four days praying, and the thought of doing it with a bunch of pastors, many of whom I didn't know, was more than just a little intimidating.

Thankfully, the founder of 4Tucson and longtime friend and colleague Mark Harris said to me, "What is it you're doing that's so important that you couldn't take four days to invest in the city? You take that much time for continuing education trips, don't you? What fills your time that's more important than prayer?" I had no excuse and signed up somewhat begrudgingly. I couldn't imagine that a couple dozen pastors could get through four days together without some fights breaking out.

Wisely, the organizers brought in an outside facilitator, Dennis Fuqua. Why? If anyone from within Tucson had led it, plenty wouldn't have come no matter who was chosen. If you've ever watched a group of pastors introduce themselves to one another, I apologize. The first

31

question is almost always, "How big's your church?" I was prepared to endure the obligatory introduction section that first Monday evening—but was I ever in for a surprise. Right from the beginning, Dennis said, "In all our structured times together, our conversation is going to be vertical, not horizontal. We're going to talk to God, and others can listen in." He had each of us share a verse of Scripture that had been meaningful to us, and then pray it. Others prayed over us. Not once on the whole retreat did we do a formal, go-around-the-circle-and-introduce-yourself exercise. And yet I got to know those 20 guys better in those four days than almost any other experience I've had.

People had prayed for many years for such an event, but Tucson's notoriously divided church had never before been able to pull it off. The spiritual atmosphere in our city changed as a result of what happened those four spring days in 2009. We've met every March since then for prayer summits, and while the group has grown slightly in numbers, the core remains the same. In our 2012 gathering, God took us to deeper levels of unity than we'd ever experienced before. On a Sunday morning at my home congregation a week later, I felt God had opened up to me new doors of understanding and given me new language to express it. I wrote down what I felt God was showing me, forming the foundation and overview for this book.

The next several chapters serve as an invitation to you to invest in Christian unity. Unity needs to progress through several significant levels for it to approach the high goal of Jesus' John 17 prayer, and Section 2 identifies five of those levels. My primary point of reference is the city, but I believe you can apply these truths to smaller groups such as the local congregation, or even smaller groups like the family or a marriage. The concluding chapters will provide a very practical look at what God has revealed to us for our city—how far we've come and how far we have to go—that you can apply to your city.

Will you allow Jesus to be your stockbroker and follow His investment advice? Will you pray like Jesus prayed and seek to live and serve in a Church that looks like the New Testament picture of a body? Will you work at unity so it reaches deeper and richer levels? Will you decide that to settle for anything less than a truly citywide body of believers loving one another and serving the city in visible ways is outright disobedience to God?

With the confidence that comes from aligning yourself with Jesus' own prayer, invest in John 17 and 1 Corinthians 12 in your city.

Section Two

Making Unity Practical

CHAPTER FOUR

LEVEL 1 — COMMON KINDNESS

*A*ll I Really Need to Know I Learned in Kindergarten is the title of a popular book by Robert Fulghum. As we seek to become investors in Jesus' prayer and Paul's analogy, the place we're going to start fits well within Fulghum's premise. Our first level of unity is common kindness—simple, basic kindness. A great deal of disunity is rooted in being unkind to one another, so the topic of practicing kindness is worth a closer look.

THE WORLD'S SERMON

On January 8, 2011, Tucson experienced a tragedy unprecedented in its magnitude for our city. Congresswoman Gabrielle Giffords was doing a "Congress on Your Corner" event when a gunman came and opened fire on her and the crowd. Nineteen people were shot, six died, and Congresswoman Giffords suffered a brain injury that eventually led to her resignation from politics. When President Obama came to the University of Arizona to speak days after the assassination attempt, "Together We Thrive" was the theme of the gathering. Truth is truth wherever you find it, and the principle "Together We Thrive" is indeed truth, whether it's gleaned from the pages of Scripture or from the struggle of a community to make sense of a massacre.

Ron Barber, Giffords' district director at the time, was also seriously injured, shot in the face and thigh. After Giffords resigned, Barber was elected to fill the remaining months of her term. While Barber was recovering physically, he created a "fund for civility." "The mission of the fund," according to its website, "is to sustain and build upon the outpouring of good will, compassion and kindness that the community responded with after the tragic event." Tragedies have a way of pulling a community together, and the hope was that the civility (or kindness) many invested in immediately following the shooting could be sustained. Common experiences, even negative ones, can create unity. Sustaining that initial burst of unity is an admirable goal, but one that ultimately needs a "higher power" behind it than mere human willpower.

The campaign for the United States presidency in 2012 was called the dirtiest and most uncivil in history. Pastor Rick Warren had planned to interview both presidential candidates, an hour at a time, as he had done in 2008. But as the rhetoric continued to spin out of control, he cancelled the interviews, citing the lack of civility and common decency in the campaigns. More people are calling for civility in public discourse. The significant divisions already in our culture are seriously exacerbated by a lack of self-control and kindness.

Civility isn't the only cousin of kindness to regularly take center stage in society's appeals. Tolerance has been the term of choice for the last decade or two. The irony is that some of the most uncivil and intolerant discourse anywhere can be found by those calling for civility and tolerance. It turns out a request for tolerance is often simply a hidden appeal to adopt society's points of view. It really isn't about tolerating and being civil toward those with differing opinions at all: it's an attempt to silence disagreement, especially if that disagreement is rooted in a transcendent source like the Bible. Don't expect a lot of tolerance if you express a viewpoint that points to absolute truth. The whole Chick-fil-A blowup in July 2012 started when some folks decided that a business owner holding to biblical values on marriage was intolerant—"hateful" was the word they used—and therefore unacceptable. We will not tolerate intolerance, they shouted, and mayors of major cities quickly went on record with their desire to ban Chick-fil-A from their cities. For many, it's easier to preach tolerance than it is to practice it.

Civility, tolerance, and kindness hardly approach the goals the Bible has in mind for Christian unity. This is just kindergarten-level stuff. *Yet that doesn't mean we should ignore it.* Many a church fight would be avoided by a simple observation of kindness. Common kindness may be the world's sermon, but the church would do well to listen to it.

THE NEED FOR COMMON KINDNESS IN THE CHURCH

The debates that rage about homosexuality have affected every mainline denomination. Personally, I've concluded that true Christian unity of the John 17 and 1 Corinthians 12 nature is unlikely to ever be achieved in such settings because the debate about homosexuality emanates from foundational principles on which unity is essential, such as the authority of Scripture (which defines sin) and the nature of the gospel (which shows how God addresses sin and sinners).[1] Remember, truth and unity are not in opposition to one another since Jesus combined the two in the same prayer. While kindness alone isn't going to resolve fundamental bedrock disagreements, it'll certainly go a long way toward limiting the casualties. When I was a member of a mainline denomination and trying to argue at a synod convention that the Bible actually says something specific about homosexuality, I was compared to Hitler—then asked by the very same people to extend a hand of friendship during the ritual ceremony known as "sharing the peace." Somehow the kindness intended by "sharing the peace" needed to work its way into the debate.

> Common kindness may be the world's sermon, but the church would do well to listen to it.

Sound impossible? It's not. The congregation I led as pastor had people in it who were recognized leaders in our community yet on opposite sides of the homosexuality divide. When our denomination proposed revising its understanding of the gift of sexuality to include homosexuality, our congregation could easily have blown apart. I've never worked harder on a project in my life than I did in leading a class called, "Coming to Conclusions Biblically on Issues of Sexuality."

---

1. In many of the conversations I've been involved with regarding homosexuality, the gospel gets confused with mere hospitality. The good news of the gospel is that God forgives sinners, not just helps people be kind and loving to one another.

The class lasted several months, and when it ended we were still not all in agreement. But by practicing principles of common kindness, we avoided any fights that would have brought dishonor to the name of Christ. A few people felt so strongly on one side of the debate they left our congregation, but they departed on mutually respectful terms.

WATCH YOUR CONSTRUCTION

One of the Ten Commandments says, "You shall not give false testimony against your neighbor." (Exodus 20:16) Far more than just, "Don't lie," the command also means, as Martin Luther pointed out, to put the best possible construction on other's actions. Here's his explanation in the small catechism to the commandment: "We should fear and love God so that we do not tell lies about our neighbor, betray him, slander him, or hurt his reputation, but defend him, speak well of him, and explain everything in the kindest way." Maybe the reason so-and-so is always late is because they have to rely on the bus, and the bus isn't very reliable. Perhaps the person who seems so rude and grumpy just found out that a family member has cancer. Putting the best possible construction on another's actions or words is practicing kindness—and goes a long way toward creating an atmosphere of unity. On the contrary, to "assume," as the old quip goes, is to make an "(insert synonym for donkey)" out of "u" and "me."

As a pastor, I had myriad opportunities to set up meetings with people where part of the purpose was confrontation. When unkindness or any other problem threatens the health and unity of the congregation, part of the responsibility of the leaders is to address it. I learned, the hard way at first, that it's always better to start with a question than a statement. If I asked a question first, like, "Can you tell me what was going on for you the other night?" I would often get a whole new perspective on this dear brother or sister's life. This would spare them a bunch of hurt and save me a ton of embarrassment for acting like a jerk. They would often apologize without me ever even having to raise the topic: they already knew they had behaved badly.

THE GRACE FACTOR

Common kindness practiced in the community of the church creates an atmosphere where grace is able to do its transforming work. Romans 2:4 says: "Or do you show contempt for the riches of his kindness, tolerance and patience, not realizing that God's kindness leads you toward repentance?" God is full of kindness, tolerance, and patience toward us. Should we be different toward others? And God's kindness actually leads to repentance. When *we* display God's kindness toward others, it can do the same thing. This is just as true whether the object of our kindness is a seasoned Christian of many years or a seeker who is exploring the possibility of a vital relationship with God for the very first time. Everyone needs kindness. If kindness is God's *modus operandi* toward creating repentance, we would do well to follow in His footsteps.

> Kindness is God's *modus operandi* toward creating repentance.

If a congregation is effective in helping its members mature, everyone should be growing in kindness toward one another. Far too often, this is not the case. People with plenty of head knowledge about the Bible use that knowledge to thump others rather than bless them. A person falls into sin and is met with condemnation rather than kindness that leads to repentance. It's often been said the church is guilty of shooting its wounded. The same sinners Jesus befriended often get little befriending from Christ-followers.

This lack of kindness raises its ugly head in more than just sin-related issues. New believers sometimes take a risk and decide to branch out and try some new ministry. Naturally, they make mistakes. What should be the response of the church community? "Way to go! You stepped out in faith!" Instead, the mistakes get pointed out harshly and the new believer's enthusiasm gets squashed. Few things are less attractive and more harmful than modern-day Pharisees in action. Jesus had far more trouble with the well-trained religious practitioners than He did with everyone else.

41

The call to kindness is one that could transform many a congregation or community. My son Daniel has a classmate, Matt, whose baby brother Ben died at the age of two from croup. His grieving mother, Jeannette, was led to create an organization called "Ben's Bells" as a way of transforming this tragedy into something beneficial. Ben's Bells is a community-wide call to kindness that has now reached nationally. Bells are made and hung in various public places, with a note attached to them that invites people to practice kindness. My wife Valerie is a public elementary school music teacher and recently heard a presentation from Jeannette explaining the concept. "Kindness is hard," Jeannette told the students, "but has actually been proven to make both the giver and the receiver healthier." Perhaps Ben's Bells should be hung on the edge of pews and over the doorways entering churches.

COMMON KINDNESS IS NOT THE ENEMY OF PRACTICING EXCELLENCE

Some congregations pride themselves on doing everything with excellence. This is a thoroughly biblical concept and can communicate to the watching world that if we demonstrate care for our facilities, our communication, our programs, and our dependability, we can also be counted on to demonstrate care for our dear guests. If musicians are expected to practice, preachers expected to prepare, and meetings expected to be facilitated well, the whole community must have a desire to improve, and therefore must welcome feedback from others. That takes an uncommon level of humility and kindness from leaders and followers, as will be examined more thoroughly in Level 4. Feedback won't always be given perfectly, and repentance will often be required; feedback won't always be received perfectly, and repentance will often be required. What is the atmosphere that best leads to repentance? Kindness.

COMMON KINDNESS IS NOT THE ENEMY OF A PURSUIT OF TRUTH

Kindness, especially from a biblical point of view, doesn't mean being sloppy with the truth. While similar words such as "tolerance" may mean exactly that when used in society, biblical kindness nowhere implies dumbing down the truth. It simply means treating one another with respect, embodying grace with others who are learning or may not have communicated effectively what they were trying to say.

If a congregation is effective in reaching out to people with the love of Christ, its unity is going to be severely challenged. Why? People don't mature instantly. When someone is born again, they're born again as a baby Christian. Nobody is born mature. They'll bring with them all their old attitudes and habits. Congregations that are effective in outreach will be full of baby Christians, and baby Christians can be expected to act, well, immature. Remember again the role of kindness? It leads to repentance. If we want to see Christians who haven't matured actually grow and be transformed, it's going to take boatloads of kindness.

COMMON KINDNESS *WITHIN* THE CONGREGATION OR HOUSEHOLD

Valerie and I took a marriage course a couple years ago called "Love and Respect." One of the main things we both took from it was a simple statement that was repeated often: your spouse is a person of goodwill. Not perfect, but a person of goodwill. Now, if you've truly married someone evil, perhaps that doesn't apply. But in most cases, you married someone of goodwill or you wouldn't have married them in the first place. In the heat of the moment, it's easy to treat someone you love like they're the enemy. Remembering that the person across the table is a person of goodwill can de-escalate conflict and prevent a huge fight.

There's an old adage that "hurt people hurt people." As I was growing up, especially in middle school, I had terrible self-esteem. My allergies were so bad I wore sunglasses indoors and my eyes were often swollen half shut. Junior high students are not typically noted for their kindness toward those who stick out, even though everybody sticks out in one way or another. I wasn't well equipped then to tap into my real but very compartmentalized faith, so the way I chose to interact with others at school was by becoming the king of the "cut down." I used my wit to come up with newer and crueler ways of cutting someone else down to size. I'm ashamed to admit sometimes I was successful to the point of bringing others to tears. When I was a sophomore in high school at a citywide Lutheran church retreat, I heard a speaker say, "There's no such thing as a Sunday Christian." This was a new concept to me. Shortly after that, I remember making the conscious decision that rather than focus on all the friends I didn't have (a direct testimony to the effectiveness of my "cut down" abilities), I would instead focus on reaching out to others who were hurting. Instead of just trying to have friends, I would be a friend. A big part of that commitment was to operate with kindness. And because it was fueled and empowered by the Holy Spirit from the outset, it worked! More than human willpower was at work, and the transformation in my life was quite noticeable. I remember very well my eighteenth birthday, looking back over the past several years with great satisfaction over the changes God had worked in my life.

At home and within your congregation, *be* the change you desire. If your congregation isn't very friendly, go to work to change it. If you don't receive much encouragement for the things you're involved in, be the most encouraging person you know. People with the gift of encouragement are gold, wherever they go.

Common kindness *between* congregations

Within any city, there are examples of congregations that are estranged from one another for one reason or another. Perhaps a key leader of one congregation left and started another one, either out of anger or distrust or maybe without fully seeking or receiving the blessing of the first church. Or two congregations might have tried to work together on a project and it didn't go well because of cultural, theological, or personality differences. Whatever the case, I'm convinced the bigger problem by far is simply ignorance: different parts of the body lacking communication with one another almost entirely. Addressing this sad state of affairs can begin any number of ways. Congregations can agree to do a project together, or agree to worship and pray with one another. This can happen top-down, initiated by the leadership; or bottom-up, initiated by individuals within each congregation. Either way, the call to common kindness will play a significant role in how effective these collaborative efforts are.

Bill Hybels wrote a great book on evangelism called *Just Walk Across the Room*. I'm aware of several congregations that have used it to effectively change their church's culture and language so that more Christians interact with more "pre-Christians" (as Hybels likes to call them). Community of Hope was one of those churches. Hybels talks about the need to leave our comfort zones and enter into "the zone of the unknown," just walking across the room (literally or figuratively) to strike up a conversation with a stranger. The exact same thing has to happen between congregations. If we schedule an event between two congregations and both keep to themselves, we usually end up doing more harm than good. Simple common kindness walks across the room and breaks the ice. Then we can let God do His amazing work of building relationships.

COMMON KINDNESS *BEYOND* CONGREGATIONS

Simple acts of kindness are often the very best way to build bridges to pre-Christians. Jesus came not to be served but to serve, and what's true for Him is true for His followers as well. The opportunities to serve in a community are truly limitless; the issue won't be generating ideas, but discerning God's call for each individual or community at any given moment. A couple of the best books on the topic are by Steve Sjogren: *Conspiracy of Kindness* and *101 Ways to Reach Your Community*. The challenge isn't in merely finding a way to serve; it's in developing the mind and heart of Christ so that we *desire* to serve.

Community of Hope "adopted" a couple of the neighboring elementary schools for many years. One was especially easy since my kids attended there, meaning that for 14 consecutive years my family had a presence at Tully Elementary. We told the principal and community liaison to let our congregation know if there were needs on campus, particularly with any students and their families. We couldn't promise we'd be able to meet all of them, but we'd do our best. The school would evaluate the families requesting help, particularly at Thanksgiving and Christmas, requiring the parents of the schoolchildren to volunteer some time at the school in order to receive help from our congregation. It was a win-win-win for everyone. One year, when my wife and I were attending one of our kids' band concerts, I was surprised and a little embarrassed when the principal asked me to stand up, acknowledging our congregation for its help. Our kindness, honestly, meant more to them than it did to us. In times of reflection, I typically regretted how much more we could've done than had gratitude for how much we actually did; regardless, we kept trying to grow our presence as a loving, caring, serving, and welcoming presence in the community.

One day, we got a call from one of the teachers of the school, Ms. Tapia, who also happened to be my youngest daughter's teacher at the time. "We know that your church cares about our kids here at Tully," Ms. Tapia said. "Would your church consider starting a Good News Club (Child Evangelism Fellowship) on our campus after school? I became a Christian through one of those clubs when I was a kid, and I'd love to help get one started here." A public elementary school was asking the church to bring the Gospel of Jesus Christ onto its campus— all because of some acts of kindness over the years.

Christians should be the kindest people on earth because we know Christ.

We examined our busy schedule as a congregation, weighed all the options, formed committees, and...are you kidding? We didn't do any of that! I told the congregation immediately I'd do it myself if necessary—and to help it get started, that's exactly what I did. But the story gets even better. The area director of the Child Evangelism Fellowship met with the principal, as per policy, to explain the club. At first the principal was emphatic: "No. Not interested." The director met with me and told me legally the school couldn't deny access since they allowed Scouts to use their facilities, but I suggested that before taking a confrontational route, I'd talk to the principal personally. Here's what the principal told me: "*You* guys are the ones that would be doing the club? Oh, then absolutely we want the club here. I thought it was a bunch of strangers."

Those simple acts of kindness led to a multi-year partnership that, as far as I know, continues today, long after my family left the neighborhood and I'm no longer the pastor of the congregation. Only heaven will reveal the full impact of such kindness.

Christians should be the kindest people on earth. Why? Because we know Christ, the ultimate source of kindness. When the rest of society calls for kindness, the best they can draw upon is human strength. We can tap in to the kindness and riches of God Himself! "Be kind and compassionate to one another, forgiving each other, just as in Christ God forgave you." (Ephesians 4:32)

Level 1 unity is characterized more by the absence of conflict than the presence of love. Common kindness can prevent many unnecessary causes of disunity, and so is certainly the place to start. Common kindness is absolutely necessary, but hardly sufficient. Kindness can be exercised and people still remain strangers. Kindness is a start—but only a start. Level 2 begins to create lasting bonds between people.

PRACTICAL STEPS TO INVEST IN COMMON KINDNESS

1. Listen more and talk less (James 1:19); ask questions rather than make assumptions; put the best construction on others' actions. Each one goes a long way toward creating an atmosphere of unity.

2. Be the change you desire—whether at home, in your congregation, or in your community. If you'd like to receive more encouragement, be more encouraging. If you'd like to feel more welcomed, start welcoming others. Focus on being a friend rather than having a friend. With God on your side, you can be the one to change the culture.

3. Make a conscious decision to view others as people of goodwill—your spouse, your pastor, your brothers and sisters in Christ at your congregation, even the person who irritates you. "From now on we regard no one from a worldly point of view...If anyone is in Christ, he is a new creation; the old has gone, the new has come! All this is from God, who reconciled us to himself through Christ and gave us the ministry of reconciliation." (2 Corinhians 5:16-18)

4. Determine to "walk across the room" and meet some other believers from congregations different from your own. If groups decide to hold an event together, prepare people ahead of time about the importance of leaving our comfort zones and being friendly toward others.

5. Remember that "hurt people hurt people." When you witness someone acting in unkind and hurtful ways, determine to move *toward* that person instead of away from them. Heap kindness on them, and pray for God's grace to have its transformative and healing effects on this new friend.

Chapter Five

Level 2 – Common Cause

In 2006, I started noticing a growing sense of dissatisfaction and unrest in our congregation. I'd been there for nearly 15 years and couldn't help but ask myself if I was actually the problem. On my watch we'd gone from being an outwardly-focused congregation eager to see pre-Christian people discovering salvation through Jesus—and all the ripples of blessing that come from such transformations—to more of an inwardly-focused congregation exerting lots of energy just to keep programs going. Sadly, I hadn't even noticed it was happening. Part of what made that change so subtle and easily missed was that all of our programs were excellent: they were easily justifiable and meeting real needs. Yet all of the congregation's relational energy was being used up with each other. Nobody had time to invest in those outside the community.

Without the energy and excitement created from stories of people being transferred out of the dominion of darkness and into His marvelous light, burnout became the norm. As a result, common kindness became less common as people found it easier to exercise

An inward-focused congregation becomes a breeding ground for all sorts of nasties.

the "gift of criticism" (a retired seminary professor attending the congregation actually claimed criticism as his spiritual gift). As kingdom growth becomes less important, people spend more time looking across the room at each other and finding more things to criticize. Like a stagnant pond, an inward-focused congregation becomes a breeding ground for all sorts of nasties, rendering common kindness rare and precious.

It took two back-to-back conferences for me to grasp what needed to change. The first was the 2006 Holy Spirit Conference, an annual event hosted by Lutheran Renewal that always recharged my tanks. This time it was more of a wake-up call: the words I heard from God were, "Step up to the plate or get out of the game." The next conference, the Willow Creek Leadership Summit, gave shape to the previous week's imperative. I remain convinced that the ecumenical nature of both conferences was a key contributing factor in helping me hear a fresh word from the Lord. The reason for our malaise? We'd lost sight of our primary purpose as a church—to GO and make disciples.

I knew I needed to GO; not to leave the congregation, but to become radically committed to mission. I'd never been out of the country on a mission trip, but announced that I would be going to Africa the following spring. I declared that it wasn't going to be counted as vacation or continuing education time, but rather as an integral part of my job. Furthermore, I told everyone I would be taking some of the congregation with me—they just didn't know it yet.

In March 2007, nine people from Community of Hope went on a nearly three week mission trip to Tanzania, no small endeavor for a congregation of 200 in worship each weekend. The common experience of mission created a deep and lasting bond between all who went. We saw joy emanate from those who'd been saved by Christ in a world where Jesus was literally all they had. We were amazed at how far $50.00 could go and how many lives it could affect. One particularly poignant evening gave our team the opportunity to decide where we would give the money we'd brought with us. We ended up supporting an amazing woman, Mama Rose, who by faith had stepped out shortly before we'd arrived and established an orphanage for street boys in Singida, Tanzania, trusting that God would somehow provide the money. It was "chance" that we even met her on this trip; it was not part of the original itinerary. The connections created by a common cause not only glued together our team of nine, but also created bonds stretching across 10,000 miles. To this day I email Steven, our driver from the trip, and even communicate regularly with Mama Rose through Facebook.

The power and danger of a transformational experience

Fortunately, we received good training through our sending agency World Encounter, which provided us practical ways to expand the impact of our trip upon our return. Rather than the experience being something that only the nine of us shared, we successfully brought the congregation into it as well. We were taught how to create and tell a 60 second story, a three minute story, and a 30 minute story. We were amazed when over half of the congregation came out for over two hours to see our pictures and hear our stories. Our congregation became the primary ongoing supporters for Mama Rose's orphanage, a partnership that continues today. Our common cause expanded to include those who weren't part of the original experience.

Unfortunately, it's very easy for transformational experiences to become a source of isolation rather than an experience of growing unity. My senior year in high school I led our congregation's high school youth group. We worked to raise money for an end of the year trip to a national youth gathering. The event was incredibly powerful, and the theme "In Christ a New Creation" is a major reason that 2 Corinthians 5:17 is my life verse. After that trip, we tried hard to "keep the fire burning" as it were, but we thought the best way to do that was to keep meeting together as a group, at times intentionally exclusive of anyone else. We wanted to share our common bond merely with others who'd experienced it. It's not hard to guess how long that lasted.

The power and danger of emotional and spiritual bonds

Fueled by the power and missional energy of the Tanzania trip, a few months later our congregation took about 20 youth and young adults on a weeklong summer mission trip into Mexico. Again, the common cause and environment created emotional and spiritual bonds. Working together for a common cause *will* create bonds, and the more outward focused that common cause is, the stronger those bonds tend to be.

Yet this can be a problem. Leaders need to exercise caution, for instance, in having men and women work side-by-side in such environments. Sometimes those bonds aren't all that desirable. The same holds true for prayer groups where male-female duos pray people through major life challenges. In all the pre-marital and marital counseling I've been involved with over the years, I've never met a couple who went into the wedding day dreaming of an affair or a divorce. Affairs don't just happen out of nowhere, especially among Christ-followers. We need to realize that the bonds created by a shared experience, a common bond, can have disastrous outcomes. Extramarital affairs and divorce in the Christian community destroy not only unity in marriage, but additionally the shrapnel wounds from an exploding marriage create multiple unpredicted casualties.

The power and danger of common cause missions

Whether the common cause is a sporting event, a cure for a disease, or parents working together for a project at a school, working alongside one another on a shared passion can turn strangers into acquaintances and sometimes even lifelong friends. One of the places where denominational and ethnic divisions within the Christian community are most regularly bridged is in common cause missions in the city—like a crisis pregnancy center, a gospel rescue mission, a twelve-step group, or an after-school ministry. When people recognize a glaring need and turn it into a powerful opportunity, many of our labels naturally fall by the wayside. Major chasms are often spanned with nary a battle: Charismatic/Evangelical, Catholic/Protestant, rich/poor, Anglo/minority, and so on. People from all corners gather together for a common cause. Often the depth of community in such groups, partly *due* to the diversity represented, is rich and highly treasured.

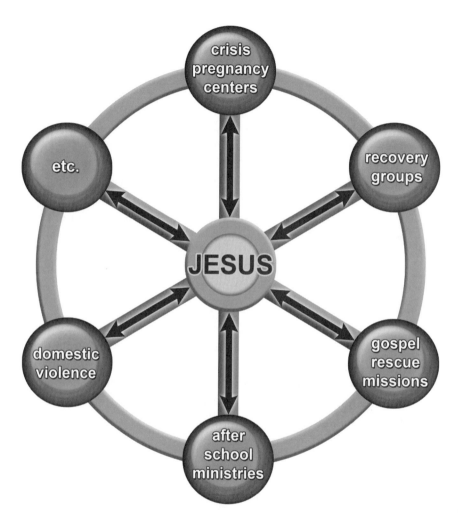

Each common cause ministry is birthed in the heart of Christ. The closer each stays to Christ, the more they discover their need and appreciation for one another, too. Distinctive missions are maintained, yet each recognizes that a one spoke wheel goes flat in a hurry.

There lies another of the dangers. Many people call their twelve-step group their "church." While it can be an indictment against Christian communities that struggle to be "real," it also reveals a tendency to elevate the common cause higher than warranted. At our citywide meetings where both pastors and common cause ministry leaders are invited, we've had to institute "no soliciting" rules. Otherwise, those repr senting the ministries would be so passionate about their cause, th. pastors would stop coming. Pastors are regularly approached by multitudes of worthy common causes, and no congregation is called to do all of them. It can be challenging, though, for someone whose life has been changed in a common cause ministry to accept "No" or "Not now" as an appropriate response. Additionally, it takes higher levels of unity, to be discussed in later chapters, to prevent common cause ministries from competing with one another and with the local congregations for the same money and volunteers.

The power and danger of being in the world but not of it

Missional communities harness the power of common causes in creative ways. As they recognize the need for disciples of Jesus to make more disciples of Jesus, they also discover the incredible resource all Christians are in and of themselves. Every believer has a unique set of relationships and interests. We can take all the activities we already enjoy—sports, art, postage stamp collecting, coffee, whatever they are—and use them to intentionally cultivate relationships with pre-Christians. Bill Hybels' *Just Walk Across the Room* does a marvelous job providing practical training in how to employ the power of common cause relationships for kingdom growth.

This can be done not only individually but collectively. Every congregation has a neighborhood school not too far away, and every school has needs. One of our phrases in 4Tucson is: "You don't have to believe like I believe to care about what I care about." Christians and atheists alike care about kids. By intentionally coming alongside others in a common cause, we can begin to function like the salt and light that Jesus calls us to be. In fact, *only* by operating in consistently close proximity with the unchurched do we function as salt and light.

Salt left in its shaker flavors nothing, and light hidden under a basket cannot shine.

The caution here is that there are ditches on both sides of the road. Christians on one side cloister together and have little to no contact with the outside world. Christians on the other side of the road connect so well to the unchurched they lose their distinctive and primary identity in the process. While examples of this are legion, let's look at one of the most hotly contested issues in our society: homosexuality. In one ditch are Christians who shout out "truth" while remaining at arm's length or worse from any actual people who consider themselves homosexual. They may be biblically accurate on sexual morality, but woefully lacking on biblical love. In the other ditch are Christians who do well to love those who are homosexual but conclude the best way to do that is to bless what they bless. The most common argument for this position goes something like, "I know 'Lisa' personally. She's my friend. She's a wonderful person." In order to love her, they feel they have to overlook or overturn what the Bible says about the issue.

Remember, Jesus planted a prayer for us to be sanctified by the truth of God's Word right in the middle of His prayer for Christian unity and love. Truth and unity are friends, not foes. The gospel itself is God announcing the truth of our sinfulness and need of a Savior while loving us sacrificially to and through death itself. We can't allow the bonds we build with others to blind us to the truth of the Bible. God's Word wasn't given to restrict us or steal our fun, but that we might have life, and have it abundantly, to the full—as God designed (John 10:10). The gospel sets people free in all aspects of life.

THE POWER AND DANGER OF COMMON CAUSE COUNCILS

Our identity in Christ is our primary identity. But that identity gets lived out in a multitude of ways. Some Christians are businesspeople. Some are artists and musicians. Some are youth and some are seniors. Some are media-savvy. Some are salespeople. Some are teachers. Some are nurturers. Some are charge-the-hill leaders. Some are count-the-cost followers. All these perspectives are part of the body, by God's design, and all are necessary.

Leadership teams (also known as elder boards or church councils, depending on the denomination) operate within this dynamic in a variety of ways as well, some healthy and others not so much. Many teams, either by design or by default, attract similar people by personality as well as by experience and gifting. These teams may have an easier time relating to one another since perspectives are naturally shared, but they can also miss out on needed viewpoints that are absent from the room. Other teams strive to get everyone at the table, but can struggle with conflict unless the relationships grow and maturity deepens. Most often, one or more perspectives end up quite isolated and estranged, causing some people to drop out of the team and sometimes out of the church completely. The impact of common cause unity is real, whether it's paid attention to or not.

THE POWER AND DANGER OF COMMON CAUSE BECOMING COMMON ENEMY

The military is probably the strongest example of both the power and the limitations of common cause unity. Soldiers enter boot camp as strangers but can leave as soul mates. Now fighting for a common cause, their level of unity is so strong they are willing to sacrifice their lives for one another. Several factors contribute to such a remarkable level of unity. The more significant the shared experience; the more stressful it is; the more involved we are physically, emotionally, and with our whole selves with each other; then the tighter the bond that is created. Combat experiences score exceptionally high on all fronts, so camaraderie is perhaps best seen among military comrades.

The military also highlights the limitations of common cause unity. Sometimes the unity created is because of a common enemy. If we share an enemy, we can become friends. I somehow don't think that's what Jesus had in mind as He prayed on His way to the cross. We certainly do have an enemy, and our battle is not against flesh and blood but against, as Ephesians 6:12 describes, "the powers of this dark world and against the spiritual forces of evil in the heavenly realms." Yet John 17 and 1 Corinthians 12 requires more to be fulfilled than expertise in spiritual warfare. There is an enemy who loves to divide and conquer, but the goal isn't merely to get better at recognizing him. It's to become closer to Christ.

THE POWER AND DANGER OF DENOMINATIONS AND RENEWAL MOVEMENTS

Denominations are a great case study in the strengths and weaknesses of common causes as a source of unity. Here's the perspective I know best. Martin Luther rediscovered the prevalence of salvation by grace alone totally apart from works. This is core Christian doctrine, but valued and emphasized in varying degrees among Christian groups. For Lutherans, it's a rallying cry, and one reason why those who have followed in Luther's footsteps can have a great affinity toward one another.

> Much is lost when common cause unity degrades to a search for a common enemy.

When that common cause, though, becomes a lens by which to identify who's "in" and who's "out," what was once a strength can easily be perverted by the enemy into a weakness. "Decision theology" is a term of derision in most Lutheran seminaries. People going forward to accept Christ as Savior at an altar call can actually be scolded, certainly within ivory towers but sometimes in person as well. Much is lost when common cause unity degrades to a search for a common enemy. Among the casualties can be the original truth itself. With regard to altar calls, there's a core contribution Lutherans can make to the discussion. If our confidence is placed in the sincerity of our profession of faith, in times of subsequent doubt and struggle we can always wonder if we were sincere enough in that moment when we gave our lives to Christ. If, however, our confidence remains in Christ and Christ alone, we're on much firmer footing. When a theological insight can be seen as a contribution to the body, everyone wins. But when it devolves into a heresy hunt, everyone loses.

Every Christian denomination began in response to some need or opportunity that was being overlooked. Even cults peppered with error and untruth are probably meeting some kind of legitimate need, or people wouldn't turn to them in the first place. How much stronger the body of Christ would be if each part of the body knew its contribution, yet chose to exercise that contribution for the good of the whole rather than the foot trying to convert the hand into becoming a foot.

There have been many renewal movements within Christianity as well, always emphasizing something that previously had been under-emphasized. Marriage encounter weekends, the charismatic renewal movement, three day movements called Cursillo, Via de Cristo, Walk to Emmaus—all have been used by God to bring followers of Christ closer to God, and all have breathed the breath of the Holy Spirit into believers. In the process, fellow pilgrims have experienced a deep unity and love for one another. But therein also lies the danger. Those common experiences can be used to create disunity when they become markers of who's "in" and "out," who's more spiritual, or who's more advanced.

Within a couple years of becoming a pastor in 1990, a couple who had been deeply moved by a Lutheran Cursillo weekend joined our congregation. They strongly encouraged my wife and I to attend, not only for how it would help us but also because that was the only way others in our congregation could attend; the pastor had to be a participant for members of the congregation to be eligible. I'd heard of Cursillo while in seminary and was open to it, but the out-of-control enthusiasm from the husband of the couple actually started to dissuade me. "You're a good preacher now," he said, "but after you go to Cursillo, then you'll *really* know how to preach." "You're already a Christian, but you haven't seen anything yet." On and on it went. My wife and I put it off for over a year but eventually succumbed to the pressure. The experience was indeed positive. Not only did dozens of others from our congregation grow significantly in their faith as participants, but I've served on a couple dozen adult and teen weekends myself. Every time, though, I've made it a point to emphasize the need to see the renewal movement as a means, not an end. Jesus is the power behind the weekend, and He is available outside the weekend, too! We cannot confuse the means of grace[1] with grace itself.

COMMON CAUSES ULTIMATELY POINT US IN A COMMON DIRECTION

Working for a common cause creates unity. But unless that common cause is large enough, the same cause that creates internal unity can create external disunity. Efforts can be made to mitigate that limitation:

- A foreign mission trip can be shared in ways that divide ("You should've been there…") or unite ("Let's celebrate what your prayers and contributions accomplished…").

- Common cause ministries in a city can become wonderful places where the fullness of the body of Christ is present, working side-by-side to alleviate a real need. As long as participants in the ministry remember that their cause is just one among many, much fracturing and frustration can be avoided.

- The power of common cause unity can be used to reach the world for Christ in natural and relational ways, with everyone an active participant, not just those with the spiritual gift of evangelism. We must remember, though, that Jesus, friend of sinners, is also the way, the truth, and the life, to the exclusion of all alternatives.

> **Unless the common cause is large enough, it can create internal unity and external disunity.**

- Denominations and renewal movements all have something valuable and necessary to contribute to the body, and often bond people together who are passionate about their

---

1. The term "means of grace" in Lutheranism is often a reference to their sacraments: Baptism and Holy Communion. The sentence holds true whether in its broad interpretation above or in a more narrow reference to sacraments.

contribution. The challenge is to remember that we're *part* of the body, not a complete body all by ourselves.

There is one cause—and one cause alone—big enough to create unity without a downside. That cause is a living relationship with our Lord and Savior Christ Jesus. Listen as the verse practically sings right off the page: "Make every effort to keep the unity of the Spirit through the bond of peace. There is one body and one Spirit—just as you were called to one hope when you were called—one Lord, one faith, one baptism; one God and Father of all, who is over all and through all and in all." (Ephesians 4:3-6)

Our common lordship of Christ has helped my marriage more times than I can count. Recognizing and celebrating a common relationship with Christ can do amazing things for the levels of unity within a congregation. Jesus Himself said, "And I, when I am lifted up from the earth, will draw all people to myself." (John 12:32 ESV) The cross is the historical and theological reference in that verse. The cross is the ultimate source of unity, because in the cross the worst of sinners are forgiven and given new life. When the cross is our common cause, new levels of unity are possible. But the verse isn't only a historical and theological reference to the cross. The same result is achieved any time Jesus is lifted up in worship and praise. When He's the focus, He draws people to Himself in great unity.

That's where we're headed in Level 3 as we seek to grow deeper in oneness. Kindness eventually runs out of steam unless it's powered by a perpetually renewable energy source, the kindness of Christ. Common cause unity creates insiders and outsiders unless the common cause is Christ, the redeemer of the world. Common kindness and common cause are sources of unity that the world, even apart from Christ, can understand and apply. But to keep growing in unity, it will require Christ Himself.

PRACTICAL STEPS TO INVEST IN COMMON CAUSE UNITY

1. If your congregation has never been on a foreign mission trip, make it a priority. Pastors, go with the team, especially at first. My only regret is that I didn't do it 15 years earlier. But be sure to invest as much thought and preparation to the return as to the trip itself. Properly handled, the whole congregation can see themselves as participants, even though only a few were privileged to travel.

2. Become involved in a local mission or common cause ministry. Celebrate the diversity within the body of Christ that you'll likely find there. Find ways to encourage these ministries to come alongside one another and alongside the church (the literal definition of "para-church," a term I've replaced here with "common cause ministries.").

3. Reflect on some of the most powerful experiences you've had. What kinds of bonds were created? Did those bonds last or did they eventually fade? Were others drawn into the original circle, or did the circle become a barrier identifying who was part of the original experience and who wasn't?

4. Be on the lookout for insider / outsider language. Any powerful ministry or experience is susceptible to the temptation. Help the group express their enthusiasm in ways that point to the whole body, not just their part of it.

5. Use common causes, or common interests, as ways of connecting congregations. Youth ministries can meet together (as can youth leaders), prayer teams, Stephen Ministries, musicians, etc.

CHAPTER SIX

LEVEL 3 – UNCOMMON LOVE

Few experiences in life have brought me more joy than watching believers of wide and diverse backgrounds come together in worship and praise. Every summer when we went back to visit my Ohio grandparents, we traded back and forth each Sunday between First Lutheran Church of Ashville and Ringgold Evangelical United Brethren-United Methodist-Baptist church. I enjoyed the Lutheran hymns with organ music, and I enjoyed the Baptist hymns with piano music. One of my favorite songs from early childhood featured the lyric, "Surely, Goodness, and Mercy shall follow me, / all the days, all the days of my life." I didn't understand it as a young child, but I liked it. I thought it was kind of strange, though, that we kept singing about three women following us around all the time: I knew Shirley and Marcy, but never met the other one. Was I ever surprised when I was old enough to read Psalm 23 and discovered what the song was really talking about!

Occasionally, the songs we'd sing at the two churches would be the same ones, though I often puzzled over why the Lutherans dropped the chorus from "I Love to Tell the Story" and "It is Well with My Soul." I might have concluded that Lutherans just liked things shorter. But then when I went to a Catholic wedding and prayed the Lord's Prayer (a.k.a. "the Our Father"), I kept going after they stopped.

Ah, the quirks of Christendom. Some churches stay in their seats for Communion but go to the front for altar calls. Other churches don't have altar calls but go to the front for Communion. Still others go up front for the offering. Some churches stand for a half hour at the beginning while singing their songs of worship, and others space out that

63

half hour in five minute chunks all through the service. Churches that baptize babies recognize the need for conversion and training, so typically offer something like Confirmation. Churches that don't baptize babies recognize the need for parents to pray for God's help in raising their children, so they typically offer baby dedications.

Given, then, how much I treasure what I've learned from various parts of the body of Christ, my participation in the Promise Keepers International Clergy Conference in Atlanta, Georgia in 1996 was like a dream come true. Worshiping with 45,000 pastors (who sing *loud*) from all over the world and all over the Christian spectrum was deeply moving. I wept more in those days than probably any other time in my life. Among the many talks I still remember, the one most emblazoned on my mind was Max Lucado's talk on John 17. He said, as I recall, "Of all the things Jesus could have prayed about on the way to the cross, He chose to focus His prayers on the need for Christians to get along." That talk was the seed that germinated and grew into this book. I remember calling my wife Valerie and telling her, "Call the whole church! Tell them they *have* to be there this next Sunday so I can share this experience with them." She did, and the services were full that next Sunday. If you didn't already know this, when Lutherans get really emotionally worked up, they sometimes smile. But that Sunday, when I shared through tears about the walls between denominations coming down, there was spontaneous applause. I believed then, and believe even more now, that the majority of the body of Christ is deeply hungry to see Jesus' prayer in John 17 answered. Pastors are often the stumbling block—as I was without even knowing it for many years. That experience in Atlanta is what it took for me to finally repent from merely being a fan of Christian unity to being an investor in it.

Two other powerful worship events in my life were experienced with total strangers. One was in 2007 in a packed church building in Tanzania. It didn't matter that I knew about ten words in Swahili. "Hallelujah" sounds the same in every known language, and I felt a deep love for people I'd never met and likely would never meet again. The other was in Mexico later that same year, and it was the same story I love to tell—it's an awesome thing to passionately express love for God alongside people with whom Jesus is all we have in common. Jesus is more than enough.

At our first pastors' prayer summit on Mt. Lemmon outside Tucson, a poignant moment has often been referenced around the city ever since. One after another, each of us took our turns in a chair in the middle of the room praying—sharing our hearts over personal needs in our families, needs in our congregation, and desires for our city. After we finished praying, others would gather around and join in, expressing similar prayers and blessings as the Lord led, yet in their own manner. At one point, our facilitator stopped us and asked this question of the people in the circle, "What kind of church do you lead?" One answered Presbyterian; others said Lutheran, Baptist, Assembly of God, Evangelical Free, Covenant, non-denominational, and so on. Then the facilitator asked the person in the circle, "Do you care that you're hearing Presbyterian prayers and Pentecostal prayers?" Of course not! Jesus was being lifted up, and He was drawing all of us to Himself and, in the process, to one another.

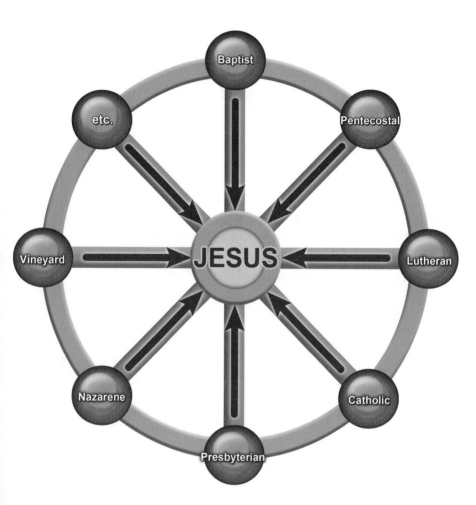

The closer each spoke gets to the hub, the closer each spoke gets to each other, too. Lutherans and Baptists and Presbyterians find much in common with one another, and even learn to appreciate the differences, as long as each are concentrated on becoming more Christ-like and lifting Jesus up, not their denominational distinctives.

Several of the pastors on the mountain those three days in 2009 were people I met for the first time. Jesus created a love for one another that is otherworldly, "uncommon" in the truest sense of the word. We've preached in one another's congregations, given one another financial help in times of need, and laughed and cried together many times since. As one of my African American brothers says regularly, "You're my brother from another mother."

JESUS COMMANDED LOVE BEFORE HE PRAYED FOR IT

The way the apostle John has recorded his Gospel, Jesus' John 17 prayer for unity is the culmination of five red-letter chapters (some Bible publishers print the words of Jesus in red). Much can be gained by paying attention to the connections between the chapters. John 17 isn't a prayer prayed in solitary confinement. It grows out of the experiences of that momentous Last Supper evening.

The scene in John 13 begins with Jesus' surprising servanthood toward His disciples. Shortly after teaching them by example, He teaches them in words. When Jesus said, "A new command I give you," the directive wasn't to be kind to one another. It went far beyond being civil, and left the instruction to be tolerant of one another's differences in the dust. The command was to *love*. "A new command I give you: Love one another. As I have loved you, so you must love one another. By this everyone will know that you are my disciples, if you love one another." (John 13:34 NIV 2011)

CHRISTIANITY IS INHERENTLY RELATIONAL

The first thing worth noticing about that command is how the Christianity that Jesus Christ started is inherently relational and communal. "Private religion" is completely foreign to the New Testament, though it's the flavor of choice for most in our society. Part of what makes this love uncommon is how counter-cultural it truly is. For example, my city of Tucson (about one million people) is one of the most unchurched metropolitan populations in the nation. One study has estimates of active participants in a Christian church at a mere seven percent in Tucson. According to the Barna Group, around 73 million adults are presently unchurched nationwide. When teens and children are added, the total swells to roughly 100 million Americans.

"Love one another" is merely the strong matriarch of a whole family of "one anothers" in the New Testament. There are over 50 of them, ranging from love one another to forgive one another, from confess your sins to one another to bear one another's burdens.[1] Lose the "one another" aspect of Christianity and you lose the heart of our faith. As my home pastor Rick Leis likes to say, "The Bible can be summed up in one word, and that word is relationship."

Perhaps you've seen the bumper sticker that says, "Jesus I like—it's His followers I can't stand." Sadly, I understand some of the sentiment behind that statement. Few sights are less attractive than mean, angry pew-sitters in action. Some of the cutting things that people have said to me in the greeting line on the way out of worship are enough to make a person's head spin and eyes leak. I remember repeatedly praying that if those comments were going to be made, that they would be made to me rather than to some other dear sister or brother in the congregation. I say that not out of a call to martyrdom, but rather pragmatism. I'd also get lots of positive strokes in the greeting line. People will say "nice sermon" even if they didn't hear any of it. Numerous saints lift up their pastors in prayer, so I at least had some counterbalance to the negativity and, therefore, the capacity to absorb some of the vitriol without bouncing it around the room. Unfortunately, unless encouragement is common and systematized, it takes just one caustic comment to virtually guarantee subtracting one from the number of churchgoers and adding one to the number of Christians who are either disconnected from the body—or worse, decide to abandon Christ altogether, as if it was somehow His fault.

> The Bible can be summed up in one word, and that word is relationship.

---

1. See end of book for a full listing of all the "One Another" commands in the New Testament.

People are people wherever they go, and the church is certainly no exception to that. If it weren't for sinners, churches would have no customers at all. Even though I have a ton of empathy for those who've been hurt by the congregation and therefore chosen to abandon the Church, I don't have the authority to amend the New Testament. I can't change Jesus' statement to read, "Love one another, unless you've been hurt by one of them." Whatever the reason for trying to fly solo, Christianity is inherently a team sport. It's like telling Jesus, "I'd love to hang out with you, but I have no use for your bride." The New Testament is so inherently relational that Jesus calls His church His bride! It doesn't get much more relational than that. No husband would accept a dinner invitation from a friend who told him to leave his wife at home—I hope, anyway.

> "I'd love to hang out with you, but I have no use for your bride."

As a pastor, one of my most important ministries is being a wound lancer. People share how hurt they've been in the body of Christ, and I simply listen, encourage them to keep talking, and say, "I'm so sorry that happened to you." Somehow it carries a little more weight coming from a pastor, though anyone can engage in the ministry of reconciliation. I pray for them and with them, thus beginning the process of helping them recover trust and reconnect to the body. Recently I had the chance to apologize to a person who'd been molested as a child by a church leader. You could visibly see his face and body language relax, and him become more at ease around the other churchgoers in the room.

My daughter Amy and her fiancé Kosmos are actively involved in their Intervarsity chapter at Northern Arizona University. They decided to actively engage in the ministry of wound healing. They created a big poster and put at the top of it, "I hate religion because..." Anybody that walked by was invited to write on the poster their completion to the sentence. Everyone was encouraged to be honest, and virtually all of them had a story of being hurt by someone in the church. By giving them the opportunity to share their hurts, healing began.

LOVE IS COMMANDED

The second thing to notice about this verse is that it's a command: "Love one another, people!" Which raises an obvious question: Can love be commanded? Pause for a moment and think about that. Love can't be commanded if it's an emotion. If you've ever tried to command your emotions, you know how futile that can be. "Be happy," you tell yourself. How's that working out for you?

Yet Jesus seems to think love *can* be commanded. In case we miss it at first, in "a new command I give you," the verb itself, love, is technically an imperative. Love can only be commanded if it's primarily a decision, not an emotion. Indeed, the word used here for love is *agape*, the kind of love most often used to describe God's love for us—God's *decision* to love us. When God so loved the world, was it because we were so loveable? Warm fuzzy feelings well up in the Godhead every time He thinks of us? Not exactly. Love is more about commitment and decision than it is an emotion. While you can't command an emotion, you *can* train your mind and your will. As you do, your emotions eventually come around to back up what your mind and your will have decided.

You may not be "feeling the love" for some of the Christ-followers in your life, and it's highly unlikely you're overcome with emotion for Christians in other congregations in your city who you've never met. The good news is that neither of those is required; neither is what Jesus commands. All you need to do is make a decision to act with love toward fellow believers, just as God made a decision to act with love toward you. Make it a commitment and consciously choose to do things that reflect that commitment. If there's a conflict between your mind and emotions—such as you know enough about the other people to know that you don't want to like them, much less love them—pay attention to other commands in the New Testament, like Matthew 5:44 which says, "Love your enemies and pray for those who persecute you." It's been said it's impossible to continually pray for your enemies. Why?

If you make that commitment, they won't be your enemies for long. God will fill you with love for even the most unlovely, because you're regularly communing and communicating with God who *is* love. You'll begin to discover that the reason they acted the way they did toward you likely has something to do with how someone else once acted toward them. As the saying goes, "Hurt people hurt people." Rather than continue a sad cycle of hatred, you by your prayers and the love that grows out of them will have the opportunity to put a stop to it—and change the course of history.

WHAT'S NEW ABOUT THIS COMMAND?

John 13 wasn't the first time Jesus taught His disciples to love one another. In fact, when teaching about the greatest commandments of all on which the entire Bible stands, Jesus said the whole requirement of the law really boiled down to one commandment in two parts: "Love the Lord your God...and love your neighbor as yourself." (Matthew 22:37-39) And even that wasn't unique to Jesus. He was quoting the Old Testament (Deuteronomy 6:5; Leviticus 19:18). What was new about this commandment was the context, summarized in Jesus' phrase, "as I have loved you." John 13:1-4 tells it this way: "It was just before the Passover Feast. Jesus knew that the time had come for him to leave this world and go to the Father. Having loved his own who were in the world, he now showed them the full extent of his love. The evening meal was being served, and the devil had already prompted Judas Iscariot, son of Simon, to betray Jesus. Jesus knew that the Father had put all things under his power, and that he had come from God and was returning to God; so he..."

If you don't already know what comes next, how would you complete that sentence? Having come from God and about to return to God, with all powers at His disposal, Jesus...

Jesus demonstrated His love for His disciples by serving them, washing their feet. The Lord of all donning a servant's towel was strikingly "new." Picture the disciples, while the only sound in the room was the dripping of water into a basin and Jesus' knees scuffling on the floor, pondering what was happening until finally Peter couldn't take it any longer. Jesus' surprising servanthood paved the way for Jesus' surprising strategy. Love serves. God, who is love, serves. That was new.

Jesus then took the familiar Passover meal and gave it a new meaning. Ultimate freedom doesn't come from a Passover lamb laying down its life, but from the Lamb of God, sent from heaven, laying down His life. Freedom from slavery in Egypt was good. Freedom from slavery to sin is better and much more all-encompassing. The Passover bread was now the body of Christ, given for us. The Passover wine was now the blood of Christ, shed for us. That was entirely new. Love lays down one's life for another.

But it wasn't only the example that was new—the source was also new. "Love one another as I have loved you" means more than "in the same way as I have loved you." It also means "with the very love that I am giving you." Again, God is love. Jesus wasn't just pointing them in a new direction; He was giving them the power to *go* in a new direction. It's the difference between a road map and a ride, a friend telling you where to go and that same friend taking you there. Jesus isn't just telling the disciples how to love. He's giving them an unending source of love from which to draw.

WHAT MAKES THIS LOVE UNCOMMON?

This third level of unity is called "uncommon love" because it's rooted in God, not in us. Uncommon love as a deepening expression of unity isn't born out of common personalities or shared experiences. Many of the Christians who are our closest friends would probably be friends even if it weren't for Jesus. We may have much in common— our kids are the same age, we come from similar economic backgrounds, we like to do many of the same things, we've gone through common experiences. That's fine, but it's hardly enough to wow the world. What we have here is an uncommon love because it's rooted in God alone, who is love.

One March many years ago Pam came to visit the congregation where I was pastor. As she described it later, "It was the strangest thing.

I was driving by, like I always did, and my car just decided to pull into the parking lot. It was as if I had no control at all over what was happening. It was my birthday, I was alone in my car, and I decided to give myself a birthday present by going inside to see what it was like. What I remember most was during Communion, just watching how much love there was in the room, and how deeply it seemed that people loved one another. I was hooked right then. I knew I needed to be a part of such a community."

Jesus isn't commanding a holy huddle, a love fest that's an inside job.

The "you" in John 13 is plural—really plural. Jesus says, "As I have loved you (all of you, each of you who follow me in somewhat unique ways) so you must love one another." And again we see that the unity Jesus prayed for, and here commands, is a visible unity with an external purpose. Jesus isn't praying and commanding a holy huddle, a love fest that's an inside job. He wants the world to see it, because when they do they'll come to know that there's more going on than just human friendship. When they see that the love we have for one another comes from another source, they'll seek out that source themselves.

A deep love for one another within a congregation can change the eternal destinies of those like Pam who come in and see it for themselves. But statistics indicate that a very small percentage of people are finding their way into our churches. Part of that is that most Christians don't do a very good job of inviting others, especially in established congregations. Dr. Thom Rainer, president and CEO of LifeWay Christian Resources, says 82 percent of the unchurched are at least somewhat likely to attend church if invited. However, he also says only 21 percent of active churchgoers invite anyone to church in the course of a year. All the evangelism programs in the world haven't made much of a dent in that, at least to date, which sadly means we're losing ground, not gaining it. According to an American Religious Identification Survey, "None" is the fastest growing religious segment of our society. No wonder Jesus' surprising strategy is particularly apropos for our age. Only when people see diverse congregations operating in visible unity and uncommon love will major parts of an entire city sit up and take notice.

NICE START, BUT…

When believers of varied backgrounds, races and experiences come together, and when Jesus is truly the focus of those gatherings, the thrill of praying together, worshiping together, and serving together can actually make it easy to set aside our smaller differences. Nobody on the mountain at that first pastors' prayer summit felt like nit-picking the way someone else prayed, or their choice of language, or how demonstrative or restrained their worship styles were. We loved the same Lord, we received love from the same Lord, and we grew to love one another. Nobody told us to be kind, and nobody had to. Our common cause in Jesus was more than enough for love to flow.

However, as good as that sounds, it's seriously incomplete. Setting aside our differences in order to focus on what we hold in common is only the beginning. At first, for the sake of unity, we have to make a conscious effort to not get distracted or put off by less-important differences. It's a necessary and noble beginning, but it's only a beginning. It still doesn't approach the command that Jesus spoke, because "love for one another" doesn't happen "in spite of the differences," as if it's an act of great sacrifice and magnanimous overflow for me to decide to overlook your flaws and shortcomings. "Love for one another" has to move from "in spite of" to "in the midst of" differences and ultimately on to "because of" differences.

Imagine the following conversations taking place in a growing circle of brothers and sisters in Christ. Better yet, have some of them!

- You don't pray the way I do! Praise the Lord! That must mean that prayer is bigger than my present experience of it. I've got room to grow.

- You've discovered a depth of worship in quietude that I can learn something from. Praise the Lord!

- You seem to experience a freedom in worship that I'd like to grow into. Praise the Lord!

- You have such a simple, childlike faith. (Insert your own "Praise the Lord" from here on out!)

- You've really worked out some of the thoughtful challenges of the Christian life, and it's obvious you've done some homework.

- Your discipleship is so passionate.

- Your Christian life is so deep and thoughtful.

- Your service is so sacrificial.

- Your witnessing is so natural.

- You've developed an understanding of sin that goes beyond the personal to the systemic, and I need to learn from that.

- You're intersecting with the culture in ways I've never even thought about.

- You tackle some of the most challenging issues with such grace!

- You have an uncanny ability to keep things simple and focus on the main thing.

- You really excel at calling people to cross the line of faith!

- I love how you embrace some of the mysteries of faith.

- You really identify with the poor and the disenfranchised.

- You're actually able to keep the attention of the wealthy.

- You've endured such hardship and yet you are so full of love.

- You're a ten-talent Christian with skills I marvel at.

- You're so bold and fearless!

- You love the Word and are so well versed in it.

- You exercise spiritual gifts so naturally.

- You're a fellow member of the body of Christ!

Now move the conversations to congregations instead of just individuals…

- Your church is such a safe place for those who've been ravaged by sin!

- Your church celebrates the arts is such creative ways!

- Your church's music is so emotionally engaging!

- Your church's music is so rich and reverent!

- Your church has so many programs and so many entry points for non-believers!

- Your church has such a family feel to it that the love is tangible!

- Your church reaches the nations!

- Your church reaches the neighborhood!

- Seniors are so honored and treasured and respected in your church!

- Children feel so welcome, cared for, and paid attention to in your church!

- Your church is willing to love the young adults even while they're challenging authority!

- Your church looks so normal and simple, I felt safe coming in!

- Your church has so many different ethnic groups a part of it, and I love that!

- As soon as I entered your church, the stained glass and magnificent space helped me immediately know that God is so much bigger than I am!

- Your church meets in a living room—it feels just like getting together with family!

- Your church reaches men and challenges them in significant ways!

> **Love for one another has to mean celebrating our differences, not just setting them aside.**

- Your church really seems to encounter the transcendent in the way it celebrates baptism and communion!

- Your church looks like a lot of the New Testament in the way it practices spiritual gifts!

- Your church is able to reach people far from God!

- Your church is able to help people mature into world-changing Christ-followers!

- Your church does an amazing job of striving for excellence!

- Your church gives people the freedom to try something new and blow it!

- Your church connects the generations!

- Your church has the disenfranchised and the wealthy in the same row!

- Your church gives hope to addicts!

If we're truly going to love one another in the body of Christ, it has to mean more than setting aside our differences; it has to come to mean celebrating and appreciating them. The hand doesn't say to the foot, "Well, I guess I can tolerate the fact that you're not a hand like me." No, the hand learns to appreciate what only the foot can do, and together, hands and feet accomplish far more than either could by themselves.

As I was writing this chapter, a Lutheran pastor called and asked if I could put him in touch with another pastor in town who has experience in deliverance ministry. That's what I'm talking about! I contacted pastors I knew, who recommended other pastors they knew, and as it turns out, the one I ended up reaching was thrilled to be asked. And, his parents many years ago had been members of the requesting pastor's congregation for over 20 years, so the request itself brought about a kind of homecoming.

Know, though, that true love for one another will go only as far as humility takes it. That's the focus of Level 4.

PRACTICAL STEPS TO INVEST IN UNCOMMON LOVE

1. Be a wound healer. Ask people you know who aren't in a church if they've had a bad experience and, if so, invite them to share it. When they're done, simply tell them how sorry you are that it happened.

2. Form a summit-style prayer meeting, either consistently or just once. Intentionally invite Christians from other congregations and backgrounds. If you want to know who's a Christian in your neighborhood, you can start by simply observing which cars on your block transport people on Sunday morning. Or if you're a pastor, invite the pastors in your vicinity, especially the ones you don't know. Have you ever been to a prayer meeting where 90 percent of it was talking about your prayer concerns and 10 percent was praying? Here's how to avoid that. Make all conversation vertical. Each person prays their concerns, praises, hopes, and dreams to God, one person at a time. Then everybody else echoes and joins in by praying for that person. It's hard to argue with someone's heartfelt cries to God.[2]

3. Form a small group and study together the "one anothers" at the end of this book. Which surprise you? Which do you have the most experience with? Which do you have the least experience with? Which does your group need to pay attention to in order to continue growing together?

4. Since love serves, grab a friend and offer to go serve a congregation that isn't your own. Be creative.

5. In my city of Tucson, Diane is a one woman force for Christian unity. She finds prayer meetings and joins them for a season, blessing congregation after congregation. If you're a prayer warrior, consider following in Diane's footsteps.

---

2. For more great ideas on how to make corporate prayer dynamic and engaging, see the book written by Dennis Fuqua, the leader of our pastors' prayer summits: *United and Ignited: Encountering God through Dynamic Corporate Prayer.*

6. Worship together with some Christian congregations that are different than yours racially and denominationally. Pray in advance for the love of God to flow. Learn how to "submit to one another out of reverence for Christ" (Ephesians 5:21) in preparation. If you're a leader, don't neglect some training upfront and debriefing afterward, to ensure that the experience leads to greater unity.

7. Have your congregation publicly pray for another congregation in your area each Sunday. Include a few sentences of description about this other part of the body and, if possible, contact them ahead of time to ask one prayer request. In my city, 4Tucson is helping organize this citywide so different congregations are all praying for the same congregation each Sunday, ensuring a very broad and diverse picture of the Church week after week.

Chapter Seven

Level 4 –
Uncommon Humility

True love for one another will go only as far as humility takes it. We can set aside our differences with only a minimal amount of humility. We can come to appreciate our differences with large doses of humility. We can break through the barriers our differences will inevitably create only if humility becomes a significant character trait.

Ephesians 4 and the Bill Cosby Bible Hour

Ephesians 4 ranks right up there with John 17 and 1 Corinthians 12 among the greatest chapters in the New Testament on Christian unity. In the first half of the chapter, various roles within the body of Christ (some denominations refer to them as the fivefold offices) all work together to help equip and mature believers. The goal is a high calling indeed—"the whole measure of the fullness of Christ." (Ephesians 4:13) The second half of the chapter is filled with great and practical instruction on living out our Christian faith in community with other sisters and brothers in Christ.

When I graduated from high school, I had no idea what I wanted to be when I grew up. I had essentially functioned as a youth pastor for my own youth group my senior year and loved it, and was heavily involved in church life, but somehow managed to miss tackling the question, "What does God want me to do with my life?" Lots of people told me I should think about becoming a pastor, but I didn't. Think about it, that is. I can honestly say it wasn't that the idea was unappealing, as it is for many. I wasn't running away from a calling. I just wasn't even considering a calling.

I went into engineering in college because I liked math and science and that's what my math/science friends were doing. It was never a calling, either. I was simply more comfortable answering the question, "What are you going to major in?" with "Engineering" than "I don't know." I've never regretted it, though I never would have chosen such a major if I knew from the outset that I would head to seminary afterwards. Thank God that Jesus is Lord and not me. He sees the whole picture when we only see pieces.

My home congregation, Spanish Trail Lutheran Church, asked me to help get a college ministry started. I tried diligently my freshman year, but most of my Lutheran peers weren't interested. After a year or so, I remember asking my pastor, "Do I have your blessing to make this *not* the Spanish Trail Lutheran Church college age group? Can it meet somewhere else and include anyone who's interested, whether they're Lutheran or not?" Thankfully he said "Yes," and that experience remains one of the most joy-filled of my life. The group slowly grew to 30 or 40 people crammed into the living room of my little house near the University of Arizona campus. We had students from lots of different denominations coming, including some Mormons and others outside the Christian community. Visible unity and love for one another, which we had, is very attractive, just like Jesus prayed it would be.

We met on Thursday evenings in the early 1980s, back when The Cosby Show burst onto the scene. Several of us wanted to watch it, so we invited anyone who so desired to come watch The Cosby Show together, and then we'd do our Bible Study afterwards. We came to be known as the Bill Cosby Bible Hour. Years later, half of our wedding party was participants of the Bill Cosby Bible Hour, all of whom remain close friends all these years later. A couple years ago I got a call from a military chaplain's wife who was attending a conference in Phoenix. Somehow my name came up, and she remembered me from the Bill Cosby Bible Hour and looked me up. She called to tell me that she had become a Christian at my house, though she'd never told me. I was thrilled—but also humbled, because in all honesty I didn't remember *her*, let alone the significance of her attendance.

By the time I graduated from college, God finally had my attention and I knew He was calling me to be a pastor. I didn't want to start over in a different degree program, and the entrance requirement for the Lutheran denominational seminaries was merely a bachelor's degree. I was a little concerned about the theological content I might be taught at the seminary, having already noticed that you can't believe everything you hear, and went in with my eyes at least somewhat open. As a way of preparing well, I decided to go to a month-long summer camp offered by Navigators right after graduation from the University of Arizona, right before moving to Ohio to attend Trinity Lutheran Seminary. A few people expressed concern that I might get theological whiplash, but I saw the diversity as a plus, not a minus.

The camp director was of the belief that you had to have a specific moment of conversion to truly be a Christian. I didn't have such a moment; my life was a progression with some clear markers along the way. I can't remember a time I'd say I didn't know or love Jesus. So day after day he tried to convince me, and day after day I held my ground. Two days before the summer camp ended, he said, "David, I'm not sure *when* you became a Christian, but I'm convinced that at some point, you did." Ah, sweet victory.

There were many lasting life lessons from that camp: Scripture memorization being one of them, the value of quiet times another. A third was the camp rule, what they called the "Ephesians 4:29" rule: Don't let any unhelpful talk leave your mouth, but only say things that build others up. That's Level 1—common kindness. But with a divine power source behind it, it's great advice for building Christian unity, or at least preventing lots of disunity.

Ephesians 4:3-6 could be the theme verses for this whole book if they didn't have such great competition. "Make every effort to keep the unity of the Spirit through the bond of peace. [Meaning that being a fan of Christian unity isn't the same thing as investing in it. We're commanded to make "every effort."] There is one body and one Spirit— just as you were called to one hope when you were called—one Lord, one faith, one baptism; one God and Father of all, who is over all and

83

through all and in all." But notice where this starts. The verses right before these say, "As a prisoner for the Lord, then, I urge you to live a life worthy of the calling you have received. Be completely humble and gentle; be patient, bearing with one another in love." (Ephesians 4:1-2)

AN ORIENTATION NOT OF MY CHOOSING

I was born competitive—highly competitive. If you think you know someone more competitive, I think you're wrong. My wife accuses me of deriving joy from beating my own kids at games. I argue in return that my penchant for winning makes it more meaningful and enjoyable for the kids in those rare moments when they beat me.

I didn't choose this orientation, or the pride that it grows out of. Nature or nurture is an open question – was I born with such an inclination? Did I learn it through childhood experiences? During the month-long trips my family would take to Ohio every other summer, we would play board games by the hundreds. Not only would we keep score in the games, we kept score of how many games each of us won. I'm not positive this was my grandmother's idea, but that's my story and I'm sticking to it. If I were Adam, I would have introduced the concept of scorekeeping to Eden—and definitely to Eve.

Oftentimes the competitiveness was with myself. I would keep track of how many free throws I could make in a row. (I still do—it's 28, in case you're wondering.) The only video games I like are ones where I can work at improving my winning percentage. My goal in school wasn't only to get the highest score in the class; it was to get a higher score than I did the last time. I didn't like to make mistakes in school; my first B came my second year of college, and it was devastating. Make no mistake, though—I was competing with others even though I knew better than to show it. I still remember the day that Leah Wolfe, with whom I was tied for valedictorian going into my senior year of high school, got a B. Oh, happy day!

Sadly, my pride and competitiveness shows up in far less benign arenas than board games and self-improvement goals. I often daydreamed of being the best pastor ever. Properly framed, that isn't necessarily demonic, but when you add in my scorekeeping tendencies, let's just say it's a good thing I learned the Ephesians 4:29 rule when I did and knew enough to keep many of my thoughts to myself. Score-keeping pastors aren't the ingredient of choice if you're trying to cook up Christian unity in a city.

If you haven't already figured out where this is headed, let me help you. Everyone makes mistakes. When you have the orientation I had, which I didn't choose, it's exceptionally difficult to *admit* your mistakes. For some reason that I still don't fully understand, I found it easier to say "I'm sorry" at church than I did at home. It was grueling to get me to a place of admitting my responsibility in conversations with my dear and long-suffering wife. It took two years of marriage counseling and some serious brokenness on my part to get to a place where I could at least be respectable as a husband. I remain such a work in progress.

Humility hasn't come easy for me, and it still doesn't. Messing up badly has helped, quite frankly, but I remain shocked at some of the ugly thoughts my mind can brew up. Jesus said it's not what we put into our mouths that make us unclean, but what comes out, bubbling up from the heart and mind. (Matthew 15:11) That's humbling. Sometimes traveling the right road will be a lifelong battle, and it will never come easy. The solution to this excruciatingly difficult journey, though, isn't to un-sin pride and then declare it respectable or even honorable. Our instruction, as followers of Jesus, is to take up our cross and die to ourselves.

JESUS, OF ALL PEOPLE, WAS HUMBLE

Jesus was able to choose the circumstances of His birth. He's truly one of a kind in that regard. He chose a poor, unmarried Jewish teenager from Nowhereville for His transportation and a cattle trough for His destination. The royalty to bring greetings for such a noble birth? Smelly shepherds and a few wise guys who were two years late. Jesus was also completely unique in choosing in advance the circumstances of His death. Of all things He chose the cross, perhaps the most sadistic invention in a human history littered with sadistic inventions. The cross is foretold throughout the Old Testament in stunning ways. For example, look at the parallels to Adam being placed into a deep sleep, his side being opened, and out of his opened side God bringing to life his bride Eve. Jesus was placed into a deep sleep, the sleep of death, and He too had his side opened, by the spear of a Roman soldier. Out of this wound both blood and water flowed, symbolic of forgiveness and cleansing. And the forgiveness and cleansing of the cross purchased for Jesus a bride, the body of Christ.[1] Jesus grew up in Nazareth (as he was being called to be a disciple, Nathanael asked in John 1:46, "Can anything good come from there?"); was baptized at the lowest place on earth, the Jordan River; chose uneducated fishermen for His entourage; rode a donkey over tree branches to His coronation; and entrusted the message of the resurrection to a few women whose testimony wouldn't have even been valid in Roman courts.

> **If Jesus chose to be humble, how ridiculous that we would ever choose not to be.**

Every step of the way, Jesus chose the path of humility. Philippians 2:8 sums it up: "And being found in appearance as a man, he humbled himself and became obedient to death—even death on a cross!" If *Jesus* chose to be humble, how utterly ridiculous that we would ever choose not to be

JESUS TAUGHT HUMILITY

This could be the subject of an entire book of its own, but let's merely visit one example, His first significant teaching section as recorded by the gospel writer and tax collector Matthew. For many years, I looked at the Beatitudes, the first eight "Blessed are the..." declarations that kick off Matthew 5, as independent statements in no particular order. I'm forever indebted to Pastor David Johnson of Church of the Open Door in Minnesota for showing me otherwise.[2] Things

---

1. See *The Cross: Finding Life in Jesus' Death* by Mike Cleveland—60 bible studies solely on the cross. The packaging isn't impressive; it doesn't even have page numbers! But the content certainly is.

were going great for the disciples at the end of Matthew 4. It's obvious they've picked a winner in this Jesus guy, who was healing people right and left. The crowds are growing and they're in the inner circle. At the start of Matthew 5, though, things take a shocking turn. The crowds gather and Jesus leaves! He climbs a mountain (hence, "Sermon on the Mount") and the disciples have to chase Him. More shocking still were the first words out of His mouth.

"Blessed are the poor in spirit, for theirs is the kingdom of heaven." (Matthew 5:3) If you've been around church much, that statement probably feels more like poetry to you than the two-by-four plank of lumber it would have felt like to the disciples. There are a couple of words Jesus could have chosen for the word we translate "poor." One describes someone who is on the street begging. But that isn't the word Jesus used. He used a word for someone who's so destitute that he can't even beg, who will die unless someone comes along and helps him. Blessed are the utterly broken, Jesus says. Blessed are the completely helpless. Blessed are those totally incapable of doing anything for themselves. The kingdom of heaven belongs to that kind of person.

Remember the story of the rich young ruler who came to Jesus saying, "What must I do to inherit eternal life?" What happened? Several of the Ten Commandments were mentioned, and the man said he'd done all of them. He had a fairly high estimation of himself, but Jesus doesn't argue. He simply says, "Go, sell everything you have and give to the poor, and you will have treasure in heaven. Then come, follow me." (Mark 10:21) What would have happened if the man had done that? We know he didn't—he couldn't part with his possessions. Luther's explanation to the first commandment would say that his stuff had become his god. But let's imagine for a second the rich man does give everything away and comes back to Jesus, reporting his success. What would Jesus have done next? "Congratulations, young man. You are the first person ever to be saved by your works?" No, I don't think so. I believe Jesus would have given him something *else* to do, because what Jesus was trying to do was help him see that he was at the end of

---

2. See his book, *Joy Comes in the Mourning*, for a full treatment of this topic. The insights that follow are visibly lived out in their congregation, at least from my experience as a visitor there.

himself. All his good deeds were insufficient. Without a Savior, he wasn't going to be saved. Humility is the gatekeeper for salvation; without it, you aren't getting in.

> **Humility is the gatekeeper for salvation; without it, you aren't getting in.**

We are saved by grace through faith, apart from works. (Ephesians 2:8-9) But here's the deal. That isn't just a theologically correct statement that many of us (Lutherans in particular) have tattooed on the inside of our foreheads. It's not enough to be head knowledge; it's meant to be a way of life! Blessed are the broken, those who know that without the grace of God they are completely and totally toast. We don't ever get to graduate from step one, being broken, being poor in spirit. Ain't broke? Can't use you.

Let's see what grows out of that: "Blessed are those who mourn, for they will be comforted." (Matthew 5:4) Mourning is showing on the outside what's happening on the inside. To mourn is literally to have integrity, to have the outside and the inside line up. Let's say it's Sunday morning, and the alarm doesn't go off, so you're running late. You jump in the car and your spouse reminds you of something you forgot to do, so the two of you get into a fight. The kids in the back seat keep yelling to each other, "Stop touching me!" all the way to church. The car screeches into the parking lot, everybody's tense and upset, you walk in the doors, and someone says, "How are you?" What do you answer? "Fine." That is the opposite of mourning. Broken people tend to be more honest. They know they're a wreck, so they don't try to fake it as much. It's actually amazingly refreshing to be in a congregation with people who act (and are) real.

Next is: "Blessed are the meek, for they will inherit the earth." (Matthew 5:5) In our culture, we have no clue what "meek" means. It rhymes with "weak" and we think that's what it entails. Hardly. It's a word used to describe the process of breaking a wild stallion, literally meaning "strength under control." Jesus was meek. Was Jesus weak? Never. He was the picture of strength under control. Moses was meek. The word some-times gets translated "humble," and the Bible says Moses was the most humble person of anyone who lived, outside of Jesus Himself. (Numbers 12:3) Was Moses weak? No, Moses was broken. He went through the whole process of being broken. Moses' strength was evident in his early dealings with the Egyptian taskmasters who were mistreating his fellow Israelites. Forty years in the wilderness revealed a different Moses in his encounter with God in the burning bush. When Moses went back to Egypt to rescue the Israelites from slavery, it was clear to everyone that God was the one doing the heavy lifting, not Moses. Those who go down into brokenness and mourning come up meek.

People who are broken and humble also do what the next Beati-tude says—hunger and thirst for righteousness. (Matthew 5:6) If you've been broken by an alcohol or drug addiction, and you've gone through some of the mourning process by admitting the problem and receiving the healing Jesus brings, you come out of that valley of the shadow of death with a new strength and hunger for righteousness and truth. You'd do anything to help others avoid some of the pain and hard-ship you've experienced. I believe this is another way of talking about being filled with the Holy Spirit. There's a difference between someone who goes to church because it's a nice thing to do, and someone who comes to worship because there's nothing else they'd rather do. That second person is broken; they know they owe God life itself, they've eaten plenty of the food that doesn't satisfy, and now they want nothing more than to love and serve God. The church Jesus intends is filled with such people.

Then comes: "Blessed are the merciful, for they will be shown mercy." (Matthew 5:7) This is the first Beatitude that talks about how we treat others—and there's a reason it's fifth, not first. People who have gone down into brokenness and mourning and then come up meek and hungering for God are the kind of people you want to meet when you're struggling. Self-righteous people make you feel worse when you blow it. But merciful people know all about blowing it, so they actually are a source of encouragement. It's the difference between sandpaper and a soft blanket.

The last three are those who are pure in heart, peacemakers, and persecuted. (Matthew 5:8-10) To be pure in heart is actually attainable. It doesn't mean perfect. It just means someone broken, experiencing healing, hungering for God and being merciful to others. When we walk that road, we also become peacemakers. Peacemakers are also truth tellers. True peace isn't holding your tongue when something's wrong. True peace is making the wrong right. And guess what? Peacemakers can expect to be persecuted, because some people won't like the truth; but that puts us in good company with Jesus Himself.

In the preamble to perhaps His Magna Carta of sermons, we get a glimpse of the church according to Jesus. And humility is the foundation of it.

Discipleship and evangelism require humility

While the visible unity of the body of Christ is what Jesus prayed for as He headed to the cross, it's not what He mentioned as He ascended back into heaven. Every gospel writer who records an ascension scene writes of the same last words of Jesus ringing in the disciples' ears as they stared skyward. We're most familiar with Matthew's version, known as The Great Commission (Matthews 28:18-20). But Mark (16:15) and Luke (recorded most clearly in his Gospel sequel, Acts 1:8) recall the same message. It was a powerful reminder that the church is perhaps the only institution on the planet to exist for the sake of its non-members. We are to "Go, Make Disciples."

To make disciples, we must first *be* disciples, growing and maturing as Christ-followers. It takes humility to recognize we haven't "arrived," that we have more to learn. The word "disciple" literally refers to a learner and a follower, and so the only kind of people qualified to be called disciples are humble people. Movement Day is an international gathering of citywide gospel movement leaders and practitioners held annually in New York City. At their 2012 event, Pastor Rick McKinley said our call isn't to build the church; it's to *be* the church. And we are to be the church wherever we "Go." Our job is not just to welcome those who find us, but to go into the world to where others are, living out a visible love, bringing the presence of Christ with us to flavor the world.

Here's a question to ponder. Assuming your congregation's preaching, teaching, and discipleship programs are thoroughly effective, how many people would you ideally characterize as "mature" disciples, fully devoted followers of Christ? If you're thinking 100 percent would be the goal, you've forgotten the "Go" part of the Commission. The church should always be interacting with those far from Christ, those seeking Him, and those just crossing the line of faith. If everyone in the assembly has been a maturing Christ-follower for some time, that's actually a problem. And if everyone in the congregation *hasn't* been a longtime, maturing Christ-follower, unless humility is the pervasive character of the community, that will be a problem as well.

You might have noticed no one is born as an adult. Well, nobody's "born again" as an adult, either. We bring our sinful habits and characteristics with us when we become Christians. As we saw in the Beatitudes, those who are bruised and wearied by life and the ravages of sin need to encounter people of mercy and grace. But only broken people—humble people, poor in spirit people—are able to consistently *be* full of mercy and grace. One reason many of our congregations don't make much of a dent with the lost and hurting is that obvious sinners don't feel safe around our pew-sitters. In extensive surveys of American citizens done by the Barna Group from 1995-2007,[3] the first word that came to mind when they heard the phrase "evangelical Christian" was "judgmental." Jesus, on the other hand, developed the reputation as being a friend of sinners. (Matthew 11:19) The difference? Jesus chose humility, while many who claim to follow Him choose different paths.

In *Joy Comes in the Mourning*, Pastor David Johnson described the first time he knew his congregation had really taken the teachings on the Beatitudes to heart. A guy came to worship service wearing a T-shirt that said, "Stamp out virginity." Instead of being judged for what was obviously offensive, he encountered the love of Christ—not only from Jesus Himself, but from Christ's followers. He came forward for the invitation to accept Jesus as Savior, tears streaming down his cheeks. When a congregation is a place where obvious sinners can encounter the love of God, the church according to Jesus has become a reality.

---

3. See *Unchristian: What a New Generation Really Thinks About Christianity… And Why It Matters* by David Kinnaman.

PRAYER REQUIRES HUMILITY

Praying together has proven to be one of the most effective ways of uniting diverse parts of the body of Christ. When various body parts are each in communication with the head of the body, they by definition are in relationship to one another, too. When you can hear another sister or brother in Christ pray from their heart and discover that, regardless of the wrapping, the content lines up pretty well with how you're feeling on the inside, your hearts are often united.

Prayer requires humility. Prayerlessness reveals a serious lack of it. Jesus shared in His incredible night-before-the-cross discourse to His disciples, "I am the vine; you are the branches...apart from me you can do nothing." (John 15:5) People who believe that Jesus meant what He said are also people who pray. People who think they can do it on their own spend more time planning than praying. Planning and praying aren't mutually exclusive, but who we spend most of our time planning with reveals much about who we think has the answers.

> **Prayer requires humility. Desperation often helps.**

The engineer in me likes to plan. I typically don't like meetings unless there's some idea of the outcome going in. But when our congregation's planning team met in summer 2001 to determine what to recommend regarding our denominational affiliation, I knew every single person around the table had different ideas. We were as un-unified as we could possibly be. As hard as I tried, I could not come up with a solution that showed any promise of success. I envisioned a very long evening with a very unsatisfying outcome. So I suggested we try something different: Instead of praying to start the meeting, how about praying *as* the meeting? Surely God's plan wasn't to blow us apart. So we decided to seek Him, and the difference in that prayer meeting was that all of us truly believed that apart from Him we could do nothing. We didn't have a Plan B. We prayed for an hour or so (a lengthy amount of time for our particular team), God revealed a path forward, we unanimously agreed with God's plan, and a few months later our congregation was virtually unanimous as well. Prayer requires humility. Desperation often helps.

FORGIVENESS, ETC. REQUIRES HUMILITY

Humility is at the very heart of forgiveness. Where there are sinners, there will be offense. For offense not to mark the end of a relationship, forgiveness is required. Only those who recognize the magnitude of their own sin are quick to forgive. This will be explored more fully in the next chapter; but, really, we could examine every aspect of the Christian life and discover the same thing—humility is 100 percent essential. For example, you can sing songs without humility, but you can't worship. Worship, forgiveness, tithing, prayer, evangelism, discipleship: following Jesus in all these areas requires humility.

CAN YOU *CHOOSE* TO BE HUMBLE?

Humility is a fruit of the Holy Spirit, meaning that it's something God does in us, not something we can do in or for ourselves. Only God can take a heart of stone and turn it into a heart of flesh. (Ezekiel 36:26) But the Scriptures don't say, "Be humble." They say, "Humble yourself." And not just once, but as a theme throughout the Bible (read Exodus 10:3; 2 Kings 22:19; 2 Chronicles 7:14; Proverbs 6:3; Daniel 10:12; Matthew 18:4; Matthew 23:12; Luke 14:11; Luke 18:14; James 4:10; 1 Peter 5:6). It's a verb, an action, something we can do that in fact we're *commanded* to do. Both the Greek and Hebrew words for "humility" mean "to go low." How low can you go? Jesus taught humility and modeled true humility on every page of the Gospels. Some of His favorite examples were children, servants, and Samaritans. What do all three of them have in common? They're low, small, insignificant, overlooked.

Paul Anderson, founder of The Master's Institute, a church leader training center, says this: "Pride dies hard. Pride has an amazingly strong survival instinct, and while I don't believe in reincarnation, I'm willing to make an exception when it comes to pride. Kill it in one form and watch it come back in another."[4] I know this from experience. There's a reason why the Scriptures use language like "crucify yourself," "take

---

4. Much of the content of pages 89 through 94 are drawn from Paul Anderson's writing and teaching, including newsletters for pastors and various sermons and seminars. Anderson led the organization Lutheran Renewal for many years, and also helped found the Alliance of Renewal Churches, and has been one of my mentors for nearly two decades.

up your cross," "die to self." If you've tried to humble yourself, you know that pride dies hard—and keeps coming back. At the end of this chapter are actions you can take and attitudes you can adopt to lower yourself. I can't promise you'll like them; I certainly don't. But then you wouldn't expect "crucify yourself" to be enjoyable, would you?

CHRISTIAN UNITY REQUIRES HUMILITY

Pride is the greatest barrier to true love for one another, and humility the greatest fuel. None of us has a corner on the Christian market. When we recognize that, love for one another keeps growing. Remember, the diversity in the body of Christ is stunning. Take almost any aspect of the Christian life: "discipleship" for instance. We could learn something refreshing and life-giving from every different member and movement within the body. To fraternize only with our own kind is to subject ourselves to a seriously anemic and myopic life.

> **Pride is the greatest barrier to love for one another, and humility the greatest fuel.**

Rick Joyner, internationally known author, pastor, and founder and executive director of Morningstar Ministries, believes the areas society struggles with most are also mirrored in the church, both literally (the divorce rate in American evangelical churches is virtually equal to society in general) and figuratively. One of the most convicting things I've ever seen is his teaching that one of the reasons our society is so violently torn over homosexuality is because the church is so afflicted with "homo-sect-uality," spending time only with our own kind. Pride is the ultimate cause of homosectuality—and humility is the only cure.

Many pastors and ministries have a desire to see the body of Christ come together, whether it's in worship, prayer, service, evangelism, or any number of different projects. While the desire is noble, the method employed often shows a startling lack of humility. Our tendency is to *start* something. We'll start a prayer movement and invite others to join. We'll hold a worship service and invite others to come. We'll create some citywide service or evangelistic opportunity and invite other partners. What's so wrong with that? It's usually about inviting *them* to join *us*. We have a much harder time getting excited about something someone else started. Even if we try hard not to take credit for what's happening—knowing that taking credit isn't very humble—the best way to not take credit is to not allow the opportunity. Go join something someone else is doing; something you can't take credit for. Celebrate their success. Make their event stronger by your presence. Get more excited about what God's doing through another part of the body than what He's doing through you, even (especially) if they aren't doing it the way you would.

At the 2012 Movement Day event, I heard leaders say over and over, "Give everything away; be a champion of the other; work on your part but act like part of the whole; the church must be a servant community." When *that* happens at a significant level in a city, they'll know with certainty God is in their midst.

That's going low. That's choosing humility. That's when we'll truly see unity in the body of Christ grow exponentially. And, trust me, we can't even begin to tackle Level 5 without humility firmly entrenched in our lives and churches.

Practical ways to invest in uncommon humility

1. Accept criticism, even when it's wrong. The first part is hard enough, but the second part is absolutely Christ-like. King David was labeled a man after God's own heart not because of his sinless life, but in part because he was willing to accept criticism, even as the king. Criticism is always humbling, so it may very well be a gift from God.

2. Serve others, not in the way we dictate or desire, but in the way God commands. Anticipate needs like a good host. Look for opportunities to go lower. Ask for help. It's not complicated,

just incredibly challenging. Instead of doing it yourself or just "suffering along," admit that you could use some help and ask.

3. Pray. The amount of your prayer equals the amount of your dependence. If prayer is not central to your lifestyle, you are not humble, no matter how many people say you are.

4. Don't complain in the midst of suffering, as if you deserve something better. The response to testing is often complaining. Complaining says you should be treated better.

5. Confess sins to someone other than God. Just confess them. Don't justify them, don't minimize them, don't exaggerate them—just tell it like it is, without worrying about what someone will think.

6. Boast of weaknesses, meaning be transparent and vulnerable.

7. Resist the temptation to start some new ministry. Join something someone else is doing. If there really is an unmet need that can only be addressed by starting up something new, learn all you can from others who've done something similar. It will honor them, and you'll avoid many of the mistakes that come from starting from scratch.

PAUL ANDERSON'S HQ (HUMILITY QUOTIENT)

Originally published in an *Especially for Pastors* newsletter

You've heard of an IQ test, an intelligence quotient. How about an HQ test? Honestly answer the following questions True or False to learn how much more you can humble yourself.

1. I am good at asking questions, and would rather ask a question than simply give an answer.

2. I have not quit learning. I have an insatiable desire to grow.

3. I am dependent on the Lord and on other people. I show my dependence upon the Lord in my prayer life, and am too dependent to let prayer get shoved out of my busy schedule.

4. I am honest, straightforward and, when necessary, confrontive. Why? Because humility isn't worried about what others think.

5. I avoid cynicism. The struggles of life have not made me negative or grouchy. I am optimistic about the future. My spouse and others close to me consider me a positive person. Humility isn't a groveling martyr-complex.

6. I am playful. I love children, and am often childlike in my responses to life.

7. I am not a worrier. I trust God with my future, my finances, my family, and my health.

8. I am slow to label people. I tend to avoid quick judgments. I don't have a serious problem with judging others.

9. I am usually good about accepting unfair criticism without resentment.

10. I can rejoice with those who rejoice, even if I don't like them. I don't rejoice at their failure.

11. I have found blessing in fasting.

12. Submission is one of my favorite words; not to just *do* it, but cheerfully!

13. I am willing to accept blame when I have compromised because of fear.

14. I regularly say, "Please forgive me; I was wrong."

15. I usually accept God's testing and discipline without grumbling.

16. I don't often think about my place, position, or reputation.

17. Praising others comes naturally to me. I am quicker to give praise than expecting it to come my way.

18. People in my church would call me a courageous person.

19. "Transparent," "vulnerable," "open," and "broken," are words that describe me.

20. I am a thankful person.

Here's the bad news. There's no grading curve, nothing that says 15 out of 20 means "Christ-like" humility, 10 out of 15 means "nice start," and less than 5 means humility is "overrated." Jesus expects them all. The good news? If you scored less than 20, allow God to humble you as you take your sin to the cross. Jesus promised He will exalt those who humble themselves and humble those who exalt themselves. (Luke 14:11; 18:14)

CHAPTER EIGHT

LEVEL 5 –
UNCOMMON COMBINATION

March 2012 marked Tucson's fourth four-day pastor prayer summit. Our numbers grew to slightly over 30, but two-thirds were people who've been there every year. November 2012 marked Tucson's second one-day pastor prayer summit, where we again had about 80 pastors together. In both the one-day and four-day settings, I had expected the summits to grow significantly in size. Instead, God had been growing our depth. The need for unity to grow significantly and dramatically in depth is the topic of this chapter.

Scripture being fulfilled in our day is a beautiful thing. I can't think of many things more satisfying than seeing John 17, 1 Corinthians 12, and Ephesians 4 all being lived out in a room full of pastors from all parts of the city:

- Believers showing one another the kindness and compassion of Christ.

- Believers recognizing that since we have the same heavenly Father, we are brothers and sisters. We're family, on the same team, with the same Lord and Savior.

- Believers setting aside their differences in order to emphasize what we have in common.

- Even better than that, individual believers coming to humbly recognize we don't have all the answers. Our part of the body is just that—one part. Other parts of the body excel in ways we never will, by God's design.

- Believers actually celebrating the differences and strengths of other parts of the body, meaning we've spent enough time with one another to actually know each other's strengths.

- All the parts of the body working in coordination and collaboration, directed by and responsive to the head of the body, Jesus Christ.

One of my responsibilities with 4Tucson is leading a monthly lunch symposium where we ask how the body of Christ in our city is responding to a specific need, focusing on a different topic each month. The very fact that this alliance exists at all is a testimony to God's work in our city. Previously, there were a couple of groups with very similar goals each trying to have a monthly meeting with pastors. The purpose of both groups was to encourage unity and collaboration in the city— but the two groups weren't unified and collaborating! Each would advertise to the same group of pastors, and often the meetings would be on the same day, one at breakfast and the other at lunch. It took some humility and relational unifying to put an end to such silliness, and out of those efforts the Tucson Ministry Alliance was born. We immediately went from an average attendance of 15 to 25 in each group to 70 to 100 in the new combined group. The whole is truly greater than the sum of the parts, just like a body is greater than a collection of limbs and organs.

When we started planning our topics for 2013, I was convinced the process was more important than the result. Any one of us could have come up with a list of topics in need of attention in our city. While the board of directors for Tucson Ministry Alliance is intentionally representative, my hope was that we could make it even more so for this planning meeting. So in addition to representatives from the board, we had leaders from both the Hispanic and African American pastors associations, along with several other ministry groups in our city. All were people we'd already been intentionally building relationships with over the past year. Our investments paid off: the laughter and unity in the room was palpable and noticed by those in neighboring offices. We began with an extended time of prayer, verbally identified various possible topics, spent some more time praying, and then unanimously agreed on the slate of topics for the coming year. All in 90 minutes. The list of topics that resulted was more complete, diverse, and representative than any list any of us could have compiled independently. No voting, no winners and losers, no positioning or posturing, just the Head of the Body Jesus Christ directing the parts of the body in perfect unity. One of the participants later told me, "In 30 years of citywide ministry, that meeting was the highlight." When a testimony like that arises out of a *planning meeting*, truly we can know that God was in our midst!

> If unity doesn't keep growing, it will retreat back to Level 1 at best.

Doesn't that sound awesome? Could it possibly get any better than that?

It had better. Unity had better keep growing to the next level, because if it doesn't, it's going to retreat back to Level 1 at best. Common kindness, common cause, and uncommon love all help minimize conflict. However, Level 3 unity, as great as it is, is unstable, because the closer we get to one another, the more noticeable sin becomes. There's the rub. Strangers, especially if Christ is their common cause, likely won't be aware at first of the specific ways sin has infected each of them. It's only after relationships develop for awhile that some of those things start to get noticed. Many people resist deep intimacy and relationships for exactly that reason; we're bound to be disappointed. The more I come to know someone else, the more of their flaws I'm going to see—and the more of my flaws they're going to see.

I remember well one particular day in my high school choir ensemble rehearsal. We had been working on a piece for a state competition and as students were quite pleased with our progress. That's when our well-respected director told us: "Now that we've got the notes and the rhythms down, we can really start to rip this thing apart. Before, we couldn't even see the smaller areas in need of work because we were still learning the notes. Now it's obvious that there are dozens of things that need our attention." Relationships have to grow to a point where some of our more subtle habits surface.

THE BENIGN DIFFERENCES

Some of the flaws we'll notice in others aren't sin, just weakness. Hands don't work very well for walking. Really athletic people can walk on their hands for a few yards, maybe; but feet were designed for walking. Every part of the body has strengths and every part has weaknesses. That's by God's design.

Some things we notice in others aren't even flaws or weaknesses—they're just differences. One of the major differences across ethnic groups, for example, is the understanding of time. In some cultures, time is viewed in terms of relationships; in others, in terms of productivity. I first noticed this distinction on my first mission trip to Tanzania. We were walking a couple of miles for a meeting that was supposed to start at 9:00 a.m. Our leader, who lived in a small village, kept stopping along the way to visit with other villagers. It quickly became obvious we weren't going to make it anywhere close to 9:00 a.m., and we didn't. And it wasn't a problem for anyone, because relationships trump productivity in Tanzania. We could argue about which way is better, but I came home struck by a couple of things: how relaxed and happy people were there, and how my slavery to the clock returned the moment I got back on the plane to return home.

What took a couple more years to realize is that those cultural differences exist within our productivity-driven society, too. Time is viewed more relationally in some subcultures than others. I've been participating for over a year with the Hispanic pastors at their monthly gatherings. They humor my lame attempts at Spanish and have always been incredibly welcoming. One evening, I was coming from another meeting and arrived about 30 minutes late. They told me, "Now you're really one of us. You're operating on our time schedule!" They explained to me that 7:30 p.m. just means, "Don't show up before 7:30 p.m." Some of our differences aren't problems—just differences that have to be worked through.

Every Christian, and every group of believers, also has blind spots. No denomination has flawless theology. I know that will sound like heresy to some, but I cite the following as Exhibit A: "Now we see in a mirror dimly...now I know in part." (1 Corinthians 13:12 NASV) Knowing what we don't know is one of the hardest and most crucial aspects of maturity. We won't get very far in a vacuum. It's going to take another person to help us see our blind spots.

Benign differences can be cultural, areas of relative strength and weakness, or simply blind spots. Even though none of these are sinful, all can divide and break relationships, dampening if not destroying the love that had been growing.

THE MALIGNANT DIFFERENCES

Many of our blind spots are unavoidable, but some are actually sinful. Perhaps we've chosen to isolate ourselves from the rest of the body, and so we don't know what we don't know because we think we know it all. That's the sin of pride and self-sufficiency: "My part of the body is so well-developed I don't need anyone else." Some groups might actually articulate that, and we would probably call them cults. Most wouldn't, but many operate that way. Ignorance isn't bliss. What we don't know *can* hurt us and the rest of the body as well. What we *say* we believe reveals less about our beliefs than the way we act. If we act like an amputated body part, what we actually believe is that we don't need the rest of the body, regardless of what we might preach or teach.

And then there's the simple, old-fashioned, garden-variety sin. Every one of us has it. We're not always going to behave well. Our selfishness, our self-preservation, our self-sufficiency, our self-centered-ness—all of those will damage relationships in the body; in denominations, within church families, and inside our homes. When the big "I" at the center of "sIn" starts showing off again, people get hurt. As Paul

Anderson says, "It isn't so much that we need to think less of ourselves, as that we need to think of ourselves less."

All of us sinners are guilty of sins of commission (things we do that we shouldn't have) and sins of omission (things we should've done but didn't). Both hurt relationships. I can say something harmful one time out of anger and another time out of ignorance, and either way relationships can be damaged. But when I refrain from offering encouragement, it can be equally damaging. In any relationship of any depth, sin will eventually wreak havoc.

You've heard it said God hates sin because sin hurts people and God loves people—and all that is true. So when sin does its inevitable dirty deeds within our relationships, we will have two choices if we're paying the slightest bit of attention to Jesus' command to "love one another." We can either press on to the next level of unity, or we'll jump off the growth chart and retreat all the way back to the beginning. If we don't press on, kindness, civility, and tolerance are the most we can hope for. Without an advance into Level 5 unity, sin will inevitably knock us back to functioning more like strangers except now with a history, a reality where avoiding gossip about the person who sinned against us is probably the most we can hope for. Sadly, not even that goal is very often achieved.

Our only hope: an uncommon combination

What we need is the uncommon combination of grace and truth. Jesus alone fulfilled it perfectly. "The Word became flesh and made his dwelling among us. We have seen his glory, the glory of the One and Only, who came from the Father, full of grace and truth." (John 1:14) Jesus was more concerned about *truth* than anyone before or since. Throughout Matthew 5, Jesus says, "You have heard that it was said...but I say to you," revealing the heart of

> Follow Jesus down the road less travelled of grace and truth in common combination.

the truths He was discussing, not just the surface meaning. Nobody trumps Jesus when it comes to taking truth seriously. And yet what was the moniker that stuck to Jesus and became one of many reasons the religious leaders sought to get rid of him? He was called a "friend of sinners." Jesus was so full of *grace* that sinners flocked to Him. The people most guilty—the ones whose sin Jesus' stand on the truth most exposed—were the ones who stuck to Him like glue. Jesus was full of grace and truth, all the time.

For us to keep growing in unity with fellow believers, we're going to have to learn once again how to be followers of Jesus, following Him down the road less traveled of grace and truth in uncommon combination. The great news about Christianity, though, is that Jesus is more than a mentor or guru, a great leader to follow. "For the law was given through Moses; grace and truth came through Jesus Christ." (John 1:17) Grace and truth aren't just modeled by Jesus, He is their source. Grace and truth came through Jesus, and because He is still alive, they *still* come through Jesus. We can learn to walk in grace and truth because the goal of the Christian life is to say with Paul, "I no longer live, but Christ lives in me." (Galatians 2:20)

When we notice another believer's blind spot, we can learn to proceed with grace and truth. When cultural differences start to create friction and misunderstandings, we can ask questions with grace and truth. When another's sin hurts us, we can do what Jesus did when our sin hurt Him— learn to live life filled with grace and truth. We can remember Level 1, common kindness, and ask more while assuming less. We can recall Level 2, and use the truth we share as a common cause to motivate us to work through our differences rather than retreat because of them. We can bring to mind Level 3 and pray for a growing love for one another that is deeper than emotion, but instead represents a decision and commitment to stay together. We can be mindful of Level 4 and come to the cross in humility, recognizing our total dependence on God in this complex relationship enterprise. When another believer's actions or inactions hurt us, we can follow the exhortation of Colossians 3:12-14: "Therefore, as God's chosen people, holy and dearly loved, clothe yourselves with compassion, kindness, humility, gentleness and patience. Bear with each other and forgive whatever grievances you may have against one another. Forgive as the Lord forgave you. And over all these virtues put on love, which binds them all together in perfect unity." As Christians, we have the most powerful power tool of all in the gift of forgiveness: "God shows his love for us in that while we were still sinners, Christ died for us," (Romans 5:8 ESV) and not just sinners, but outright enemies. (Romans 5:10) Even being sinned against doesn't need to halt our relationships.

Speak the truth in love

For nearly two decades I've used a ten-step communication guideline in all my pre-marriage and marriage counseling (see end of the chapter). The fourth guideline is "Speak the truth in love," taken from Ephesians 4:15: "Speaking the truth in love, we will in all things grow up into him who is the Head, that is, Christ." I've told every couple I've counseled that, of all the communication guidelines, this one is the hardest to do well—because there are so many different ways to blow it! The first word is "speak," and more than half of us are guilty already. When something happens that's harmful or hurtful, we don't say anything. We keep the hurt to ourselves, thinking that's what it means to be a lover of peace. Keeping the peace doesn't mean keeping quiet! "Peace" in the Bible is always closely related to its Hebrew roots, meaning *shalom*, wellness and wholeness. Peace isn't the absence of conflict but the presence of health. Keeping quiet is often the opposite of keeping the peace.

Since most of us are prone to bottle it up, when we finally do speak, it isn't the truth that we say but an exaggeration. "You always..." "You never..." Really? No, not really. For a long time when our kids were young, we had a sign in the house with the words "always" and "never" with a circle drawn around it and a diagonal line drawn through it. Either word almost always becomes an exaggeration. Even if the words we speak aren't exaggerated, if we've bottled up things for any length of time, the emotional intensity of our statement will likely be exaggerated.

But even if we pass the first two tests by raising the issues that need to be raised and speaking the truth without exaggeration, it's an art form of almost unachieved heights to be able to speak the truth *in love*, so that the other person knows without a doubt we're for them and not against them. That's what Jesus accomplished with unsurpassed prowess. He told the woman at the well in John 4 the truth, the whole truth, and nothing but the truth—in stark, blunt terms. "You're right, you don't have a husband. You've had five husbands, and you're shacking up with the guy you've got now. You have spoken correctly." And yet this woman wasn't repulsed by Jesus at all; she became one of the

> Speaking the truth in love is so hard because there are so many ways to blow it.

most successful evangelists in all of the Gospels. (John 4:28-30) Jesus' truth-speaking was as full and complete as His grace-living. Jesus exuded grace out of every pore of His being.

We can grow in this, too! We can learn to speak the truth in love with our fellow Christians—if we don't forget what we discovered in Level 3: our fellow believer prays to the same Father I do; loves the same Lord I do; sings in the same choir; serves the same Master; rows in the same boat. If we can remember that we hardly have it all together ourselves, we can learn to raise the issues that need to be raised yet do it as a learner and not just an instructor, as a fellow traveler going down the same road and equally in need of grace and truth in our own lives. Love for one another goes only as far as humility takes it, and nowhere does humility (or the lack of it) show more forcefully than in the way we confront and receive confrontation. "Brothers and sisters, if someone is caught in a sin, you who live by the Spirit should restore that person gently. But watch yourselves, or you also may be tempted. Carry each other's burdens, and in this way you will fulfill the law of Christ. If anyone thinks they are something when they are not, they deceive themselves." (Galatians 6:1-3 NIV 2011)

So needed, yet so lacking

Because this uncommon combination of grace and truth is so rare, the body of Christ remains so immature. Speaking the truth in love is vital to the body maturing as Jesus intends, "so that the body of Christ may be built up until we all reach unity in the faith and in the knowledge of the Son of God and become mature, attaining to the whole measure of the fullness of Christ." (Ephesians 4:12-13)

How well do we measure up? Rather poorly. Read this and weep: "When asked to identify their activities over the last 30 days, born-again believers were just as likely to bet or gamble; visit a pornographic website; take something that did not belong to them; consult a medium or psychic; physically fight or abuse someone; have consumed enough alcohol to be considered legally drunk; have used an illegal, nonprescription drug; have said something to someone that was not true; have gotten back at someone for something he or she did; and to have said mean things being another person's back."[1] Statistically we Christ-followers aren't following Christ at all. We reflect the world more than we illuminate it. We favor the world instead of flavoring it.

We can cite shortcomings at every level of unity that contribute to this sorry state of affairs. The church has a tendency to shoot its wounded rather than being kind and compassionate to them. Our common causes are commonly way too small, causing us to divide up in corners rather than pull on the same end of the rope. We isolate and live in a silo state of existence rather than breaking out and loving one another deeply enough to discover and come to appreciate one another's strengths and assets. Humility is hardly the most common character trait of Christ-followers. Yet in all of these areas we can cite examples of success, too. There have been instances where unity has taken place in each of the levels previously covered. But how often have you personally experienced a group that loved one another well enough to point out one another's blind spots, speak the truth in love when sin rears its ugly head, and openly desire others to do the same for them? Not just once, but consistently? Has it ever happened in your lifetime for any length of time? So many character deficiencies in the body of Christ never get addressed, and if they do, they never get healed.

---

1. See the article "American Lifestyles Mix Compassion and Self-Oriented Behavior" (February 5, 2007) at www.barna.org.

What's far more common than brothers and sisters in Christ speaking the truth in love to one another and reconciling their differences? Church splits—and not just the really public kind where lots of people leave one congregation and join another. More often, people quietly pack up their bags and move down the road to the next congregation rather than address the issues that need attention. And when the issues *are* raised, it's rare that the other person receives confrontation with humility and a desire to learn and grow.

It's well documented that the divorce rate for second or third marriages is far greater than for first marriages. One of the reasons for this is that we bring all the baggage we brought with us into the first marriage into subsequent ones...and then add to it along the way. When conflicts arose in our first marriage, God was trying to teach us something. If grace and truth could be dispensed and received consistently, we'd learn our lessons in the relationships we have rather than facing many of the same issues and challenges with somebody new. It's been said God is very gracious with us—if we fail a test the first time, it's a guarantee we'll get a retake, a second chance at learning our lessons through the tests that come our way.

The only way forward is to cultivate the uncommon combination of grace and truth. The only way we'll see the body of Christ begin to mature is if we begin following in Jesus' footsteps as people full of grace and truth.

GRACE UPON GRACE

The very nature of the beast is that we won't do this perfectly or consistently. We'll raise some issues and ignore others because we all have blind spots, and if others care enough for us to invest in the relationship by risking a confrontational word with us, we won't always receive it well. We'll allow the devil a foothold by overreacting in one direction or the other, not only failing to learn the lessons God prepared for us, but making it likely that the person doing the confronting will think twice about taking such a risk the next time. We need grace with each other. We can't possibly improve without it.

Here is the really good news. Grace is our calling card as Christians! If there's one thing Christians can offer to the world, its grace. We can learn to apply grace to every manifestation of conflict and challenge in our relationships.

A couple years ago I was meeting with a group of people who were starting a new congregation. There had been a conflict in the denomination over the authority of Scripture as applied to the topic of homosexuality, among other things, and resolution was impossible. The group leaving included most of the leaders of the congregation. As they discussed names for the new congregation, I jokingly suggested, "'Type A' Lutheran Church." I knew many of these leaders, and knew they were going to have a unique challenge among churches: more leaders than followers, more people wanting to get in the game than positions presently available. My message to them was to memorize and liberally apply a simple phrase: "Extra Grace Required." Some would be hurting over leaving behind an old congregation, so extra grace required. Some would be disappointed their ideas weren't the ones accepted, so extra grace required. This was uncharted territory for them and mistakes would be made, so extra grace required. With God all things are possible, and grace is His specialty.

> **Grace is our calling card as Christians.**

Ripples in a really big pond

As technology advances in more areas, interpersonal communication skills become more anemic. Emailing, texting, and Twittering are not the same thing as face-to-facing. We get less and less practice at what we need more and more.

The closest of all human relationships is a marriage. The increasing divorce rate reveals our decreasing communication proficiencies. If marriage is the high point of human intimacy and yet so seriously challenged, how much harder will it be to work through challenges in other relationships? There are hundreds of interpersonal relationships at play in even the smallest of congregations, and there are only a couple of options. One is that the relationships never develop and the congregation remains largely a collection of strangers. A second is that conflict surfaces and some leave. The best option—and the only option that answers Jesus' John 17 prayer—is to combine grace and truth in our interactions with one another. Yet the primary audience of the New Testament isn't individuals or individual congregations, but *all the Christians in a city*. What an incredibly high calling: to get to know believers from other churches, traditions, and ethnicities well enough that when conflicts arise we persevere with grace and truth.

Over the last year I've enjoyed developing a closer relationship with Warren Anderson, one of the African American pastors who is a leader in our community. A few months ago, our relationship had become close enough that he took a risk by speaking the truth in love. "Dave, it seems to me and many of my brothers that there was a lot more talk from the evangelical community about praying for the president of our country when it was Bush than now that it's Obama." Ouch. I didn't want to hear that, and my first internal reaction was to be defensive. Thankfully, the Spirit trumped my flesh and I said something like, "Tell me more." Out of that conversation, we decided to invite key pastors in both the African American and the Anglo communities to get together—and talk politics. Any guess how challenging that might be in October 2012, one month before the most hotly-contested American election on record?

With much prayer and careful selection of the participants, we proceeded with our first meeting. Warren told me a few of the pastors he'd invited expressed serious doubt about whether there would be any value in such a meeting. One chose to share that reluctance verbally toward the end of our first time together, saying he almost didn't come because he was certain nothing would be accomplished. Yet everyone in the room had a desire to listen and learn from one another, and significant healing resulted. We met again the week after the election, and the results were the same—more growth, more love, more unity, and more blind spots revealed. As of this writing, further meetings have been scheduled, and I'm certain the challenges will only increase as we delve deeper into much needed topics of conversation.

Yet this is the hope of the world! I have no confidence the Republican and Democratic parties will ever reconcile their differences. I don't see how that's possible without Christ front and center. Yet what would happen if Christians in both political parties learned how to truly speak the truth in love to one another? Here's what could happen: African American and Anglo Christians could lead the way in bridging the massive racial gap in American politics. Latino and Anglo Christians could lead the way in bringing about desperately-needed immigration reform. Differing economic policies could be approached from biblical vantage points that include both human freedom and concern for the poor. Local problems often get approached differently by business leaders, government leaders, and church leaders. If Christians from each specialty led the way in learning how to dialogue together, our "salt and light" mandate as Christians would resolve some of our cities' most complex problems. And the list goes on and on. As Rick Joyner often states, "Our problems as a nation are now more complex than any mere humans will be able to solve. Thankfully, we have a God."

Christian unity has to make it through Level 5, the uncommon combination of grace and truth, for the world to truly take notice. Until the world notices, we haven't arrived yet. We haven't yet answered Jesus' prayer or fulfilled His surprising strategy. But in a world that's never been more divided, I can't imagine a more promising strategy than the one Jesus has already provided for us. Who better than believers can point to a common cause bigger than the whole world: the One who created the whole world? Who can draw from a greater source of love than God Himself, who *is* love? Who would be better equipped to champion humility in the midst of vexing challenges than those saved by the blood of Jesus? Who else will embody Christ Jesus, full of grace of truth, if not us?

PRACTICAL SUGGESTIONS FOR INVESTING IN THE UNCOMMON COMBINATION OF GRACE AND TRUTH

1. Take some time to examine past conflicts. Possible conflict sources include "benign" differences: cultural differences; one person or group's strength meeting another's weakness; and blind spots,

unexamined areas that are now being exposed. "Malignant" differences include blind spots existing out of isolation or pride, sins of commission, and sins of omission. What was the source of the conflict? What happened after the conflict surfaced?

2. Take some time to examine current conflicts in the same manner. Has anyone "spoken the truth in love" yet? If so, how is it going? If not, what's your responsibility?

3. If you can't think of any conflicts or challenges to unity in your congregation or city, examine whether you've invested enough time and energy into building relationships. If the relationships are deep at all, differences will become apparent and conflict is inevitable.

4. Where are some of the obstacles to unity in your city? These could include leaders who preach against other pastors or denominations; congregations or groups who insist on isolating; and individuals or groups who sacrifice either grace or truth in their pursuit of the other one. Pray about which of these God is calling you to address.

5. Remember next that not every absence of truth is your responsibility to address. If it is your responsibility, your first task is to build a relationship that will be strong enough to handle the conversation. What character deficiencies or blind spots are you aware of in others around the city or congregation? Are you willing to get to know the other person well enough to convince them of your love before you raise the needed topic?

6. Who has been particularly effective in your life at speaking the truth in love? If you don't know anyone, ask others who they know. Then make some time to interview that person and find out what they've learned along the way that has made them effective.

COMMUNICATION GUIDELINES

God values communication very highly. Besides the eighth commandment which addresses the topic, we also read that life and death, blessings and curses are found in the way in which we communicate. Many of us know this from personal experience, both positive and negative, even aside from Scripture. (Deuteronomy 30:19, Proverbs 18:21, Proverbs 25:11, James 3:8-10)

GUIDELINES

1. Be a ready listener, and do not answer until the other person has finished talking. (Proverbs 18:13, James 1:19)

2. Be slow to speak. Think first. Don't be hasty in your words. Choose your words carefully so that they will more likely be heard and accepted. (Proverbs 10:19, Proverbs 15:23, Proverbs 15:28, Proverbs 17:28, Proverbs 21:23, Proverbs 29:20)

3. Don't use silence to frustrate the other person. (Matthew 18:15, Ephesians 4:26-27)

4. Speak the truth in love. Don't exaggerate. (Galatians 6:1, Ephesians 4:15,25)

5. Don't quarrel. Disagreeing does not need to be quarreling. (Proverbs 17:1, Proverbs 17:14, Proverbs 20:3, Ephesians 4:31)

6. Don't respond out of anger. Use a soft and kind response. (Proverbs 12:18, Proverbs 14:29, Proverbs 15:1,18; Proverbs 29:11, Colossians 3:12)

7. Words have value. Avoid nagging and flattery. (Proverbs 12:19, Proverbs 19:13, Proverbs 26:28, Proverbs 28:23)

8. Ask for forgiveness. Forgive the other person. (Proverbs 17:9, Ephesians 4:32, Colossians 3:13, James 5:16)

9. Use your words to encourage and build up. (Romans 12:17, Ephesians 4:29, Colossians 3:21, 1 Thessalonians 5:11)

10. Pay particular attention to the other's interests. (Galatians 2:20, Philippians 2:1-4)

I/we agree to follow these guidelines, and pray for God's guidance and forgiveness:

Name: _____ Date: _____

Name: _____ Date: _____

For a printed version of these guidelines, go to
www.jesussurprisingstrategy.com

CHAPTER NINE

OUR COMMONWEALTH IN HEAVEN, HERE ON EARTH

Many times in my life, God has said to me, "Here's your next step. If you're waiting to obey Step One until you know what Step Two is, you're going to wait a long time, because I usually reveal things one step at a time." When I resigned from my position as pastor at the congregation I'd led for over 20 years, I did so because I knew that's what God was telling me to do. He was quite clear that I had two choices: obedience or disobedience. I would've liked to know what was coming next, and believe me, my wife would have, too. But waiting until achieving clarity on Step Two wasn't one of the choices.

God, of course, works well in advance of us. He was already stirring up conversations for what would become my next ministry employment before I knew my current one was about to end. In hindsight, things clear up quite a bit. But in the moment, we walk by faith, not by sight. When you're walking downtown in a city with a significant skyline, the best way to find out what's around the corner is to walk to the corner. Whole new panoramas open up when we keep moving.

Through my present position as director of the church domain of 4Tucson, these five levels of unity became evident. And they are levels, in that each one builds on the previous one. They're actually more like ripples in a pond, concentric circles, than chapters in a book, because we don't get to shut the previous chapter as we move on to the next one. If we've learned to truly love one another to the point of celebrating the unique gifts each part of the body brings, it doesn't mean we can close the book on kindness. Familiar truths will demand new attention over and over again. Less important than learning new things will likely be learning new *ways* to put into practice truths we've been familiar with for many years. It calls to mind a conference I attended where two keynote speakers both made reference to needing to reread their own books because they'd forgotten to put into practice much of what they'd learned previously.

I imagine there are additional levels of unity yet to be experienced here in this life, before we get to heaven. Frankly, I don't know what they are, because I've never consistently lived out what I already know long enough to discover them. Like my downtown analogy, if I am to learn what's around the next corner, I'll have to walk to the end of the block I'm on right now. As the lyrics to the song *Forever Reign* declare, "You are more / You are more than my words will ever say."

UNITY LINKED TO MATURITY

Let's return to Ephesians 4. It begins with a passionate appeal from the apostle Paul to live a life worthy of the calling we've received. He explains that a worthy life includes humility, patience, and love, all working together to create unity: one body, one Spirit, one hope, "one Lord, one faith, one baptism; one God and Father of all, who is over all and through all and in all." (Ephesians 4:6)

This unity does not mean uniformity. "To each one of us grace has been given as Christ apportioned it." (Ephesians 4:7) This grace means that different members of the body carry out different roles and functions, such as apostles, prophets, evangelists, pastors, and teachers. Rather than seeing each of those as different roles within a congregation or denomination, I believe Paul was thinking of a citywide church, with different parts of the body excelling at leadership, at the prophetic, at evangelism, at caring for the brokenhearted, and at teaching the Word of God.

Such an understanding totally changes our strategic approach to ministry, both in our city as well as in our local congregation. After Paul lists these five spiritual gifts/roles/offices, he states their purpose: "To prepare God's people for works of service, so that the body of Christ may be built up until we all reach unity in the faith and in the knowledge of the Son of God and become mature, attaining to the whole measure of the fullness of Christ." (Ephesians 4:12-13)

Our lack of unity and our immaturity go hand in hand. It simply isn't a faithful option to leave our level of unity to chance while we focus on maturing and helping our congregation to mature. If we're not making "every effort to keep the unity of the Spirit" (Ephesians 4:3), if we're not intentionally investing in unity, we're buying immaturity. And mixed in with immaturity will likely be some heresy, too—seriously underdeveloped doctrine or practice.

> **If we're not intentionally investing in unity, we're buying immaturity.**

Richard Foster, most well-known for his book *Celebration of Discipline*, later wrote *Streams of Living Water: Celebrating the Great Traditions of Christian Faith.* Ponder his chapter headings:

- The Contemplative Tradition: Discovering the Prayer-Filled Life.

- The Holiness Tradition: Discovering the Virtuous Life.

- The Charismatic Tradition: Discovering the Spirit-Empowered Life.

- The Social Justice Tradition: Discovering the Compassionate Life.

- The Evangelical Tradition: Discovering the Word-Centered Life.

- The Incarnational Tradition: Discovering the Sacramental Life.

What happens when those streams are kept isolated from one another? It's worse than when the world is deprived of a mighty river. When the various streams of Christian faith remain isolated from one another, *each one inevitably gets polluted.* We can't approach the items above like a trip to the grocery store (I'll take two pounds of

Charismatic Tradition, but I'll pass on Holiness…too expensive). The Word-Centered Life without Compassion? Not pretty, but all too familiar. Social Justice without being Prayer-Filled? Either it won't be rightly motivated, or it won't last. Apart from Christ we can do nothing.

On my first sabbatical in 1998 one of the books I read was *Empowered Evangelicals: Bringing Together the Best of the Evangelical and Charismatic Worlds* by Rich Nathan and Ken Wilson. I absolutely loved it! It spoke to exactly the world I was living in within my own congregation. We became quite a unique place—a sacramental Lutheran church with a high view of Scripture and evangelism, which also embraced the charismatic movement. But as I'm discovering now, we were still missing out on many of the rich streams in the faith in which other congregations in our city excel.

And so I'm reminded yet again of Paul's citywide analogy. No one part of the body will ever become the whole body! No one congregation, or cluster/denomination/association of congregations, will ever encompass the whole body. Only the whole body can be the whole body! The goal isn't nearly as much to try to appropriate every strength out there and bring it into your own congregation, as it is to unify and partner with the other parts that excel where you lack.

Unity linked to prayer

How much unity or maturity within the body of Christ can reasonably be expected here on earth? Only in heaven will sin cease to have its divisive effects. Sinners, then, are going to find unity seriously elusive. Just when it's at your fingertips, something happens and messes it up again.

We can look forward to our eventual full and unmitigated citizenship in the commonwealth of heaven; but Jesus taught us to pray heaven down to earth—to ask for His kingdom to come and His will to be done right here in the body of Christ in our city, just like it will be one day in heaven where sin no longer separates. Oh, what a glorious day! Oh, what joy and rapture that day will bring with it! Yet when

Jesus taught His disciples, He taught them not to relegate such rapture to a future time. He taught them to actively pray it into existence here and now.

Not only did He teach His disciples to do this, He did it Himself! It's what Jesus was praying for as He headed to the cross! "My prayer is not for (these first century believers) alone. I pray also for those who will believe in me through their message, that all of them may be one, Father, just as you are in me and I am in you. May they also be in us so that the world may believe that you have sent me. I have given them the glory that you gave me, that they may be one as we are one. I in them and you in me. May they be brought to complete unity to let the world know that you sent me and have loved them even as you have loved me." (John 17:20-23)

> Jesus was praying His experience of heaven down into His experience with very imperfect disciples.

Nowhere in this prayer do I get the impression that Jesus' surprising strategy was merely to paint a picture of heaven. Jesus was praying His experience of heaven—the perfect unity within the Godhead—down into His experience with a very imperfect crew of followers.

Bill Johnson, pastor of Bethel Church in Redding, CA and author of *When Heaven Invades Earth,* teaches not to let our present level of experience cause us to water down what the Word actually says. When what the Bible teaches doesn't match our experience, we should pray for God to enhance our experience rather than diminish His Word. Jesus prayed for complete, heavenly unity among very incomplete, earthy disciples. I think He meant it.

I experienced a taste of it one day as I was meeting with a Hispanic brother to plan an upcoming citywide forum around the theme, "How is the body of Christ in our city responding to the topic of immigration?" Immigration is a hot topic in our nation, but you can put that truth on steroids when you think about southern Arizona. This brother has experienced racial profiling firsthand, no matter what the laws say are supposed to happen. He knows plenty of families that have been split apart by deportation, and has quite a personal story to tell about the subject. He brought a passionate perspective to the table—a needed perspective. Yet he also had the humility to recognize the valid points coming from the other side of the spectrum. He was a contributor to unity in this discussion, both by what he shared and by the way he listened. Here's what he told me: "My Hispanic ethnicity didn't die for me; only Jesus did that." When it comes to which is more important, it's no contest.

Unity linked to Bible reading

Read through the New Testament letters from a citywide perspective and you discover something new almost every day. I read through 1 John recently, and these verses jumped out at me, all from the New Living Translation.

- "This old commandment—to love one another—is the same message you heard before. Yet it is also new. Jesus lived the truth of this commandment, and you also are living it. For the darkness is disappearing, and the true light is already shining." (1 John 2:7-8) Loving one another is an old message, but loving the whole body through the whole city is new. And in the process, more light shines.

- "Anyone who does not live righteously and does not love other believers does not belong to God." (1 John 3:10) That sounds pretty strong to me!

- "Dear children, let's not merely say that we love each other; let us show the truth by our actions." (1 John 3:18) We can't just be fans of Christian unity; we need to invest in it by our actions.

- "And this is his commandment: We must believe in the name of his Son, Jesus Christ, and love one another, just as he commanded us." (1 John 3:23) Visible citywide unity is a command!

- "No one has ever seen God. But if we love each other, God lives in us and his love is brought to full expression in us." (1 John 4:12) It isn't only the world that benefits; we do, too! Visible unity and love flowing between believers is both Jesus' surprising strategy for revealing God's loving nature to the world, and the way we'll experience His love most completely ourselves, on a personal level.

This passion to see John 17 fulfilled is now leading to new insights into the Old Testament as well. I've done various "read through the Bible in a year" programs most years of my adult life, partly because the Word is always living and active and new. Yesterday I noticed this: Jacob in Genesis 32 is preparing to meet his estranged brother Esau, who he hasn't seen in 20 years, the same brother who wanted Jacob dead upon last report. No surprise—Jacob is wrestling with God. The surprise is that he *literally* wrestled with God. After the experience, he called the place Peniel, which literally means "face of God." Close encounters with God are vital to our faith journeys, and they come in a variety of packages.

But God won't allow our intimate experiences with Him to take up permanent residence only in the heavens. He always translates them back down to earth. When Jacob actually met Esau, here's what he said: "To see your face is like seeing the face of God, now that you have received me favorably." (Genesis 33:10) Love for God always translates into love for people, even people we've wronged or people who've wronged us. That's the message of 1 John, too.

This year's Bible reading plan also recently had me in Acts 1:8-11. That passage, along with the Great Commission message found in both Matthew's and Mark's ascension scenes, remind us that "love for one another" can never be merely an inside job. It's always "so that the world may know." Mission is the ultimate mandate. But visible unity is the strategy for accomplishing the mandate. And it's not an optional strategy, either, but a mandate in its own right.

UNITY LINKED TO A SECOND REFORMATION

Many books have been written about our current age as a second reformation, as sweeping in its scope as the first reformation nearly

500 years ago. Just like the printing press propelled communication forward in unprecedented fashion, so today's Internet and social media are doing the same thing. The communication revolutions in both ages help carry the spiritual revivals farther and faster than they could have spread even a generation earlier.

> # The second reformation is returning ministry to the people.

The first reformation returned the Bible to the people. Embedded in it was the seed of the second reformation—Luther's principle of the priesthood of all believers, that all Christians are priests and ministers. But not until now are we seeing that second reformation truly take root. The second reformation is returning *ministry* to the people. For arguably 1,700 years, ministry has largely been the milieu of the professionals, those either appointed by the state or employed by the people. The growth of the church has seriously been hampered by that reality. The parts of the world where Christianity is growing the fastest have the least identifiable professional castes for any of several reasons: because it's illegal, because formal education and training is hard to attain, or because the rank and file Christians are spreading the message too fast for the establishment to keep up. Much of Section 3 will involve yet another aspect of returning ministry to the people: defining ministry beyond the realms of the church.

Could it be that John 17 also reveals Jesus' surprising strategy for returning ministry to the people? Is it possible that only as the body of Christ strengthens its connections will the rapidly growing Church in the developing world avoid serious theological and practical pitfalls? Ponder the possibility that the approximately 100 million Americans who identify themselves as Christians, yet remain completely cut off from the body, have in fact been following the pastors' lead all along— by remaining isolated. Perhaps only as pastors prioritize praying and worshiping and serving with other pastors will the unchurched masses in our country find reason and desire to do the same thing.

Unity linked to the "end of the age" harvest

Matthew 13:24-30 contains a remarkable parable: "The kingdom of heaven is like a man who sowed good seed in his field. But while everyone was sleeping, his enemy came and sowed weeds among the wheat, and went away. When the wheat sprouted and formed heads, then the weeds also appeared. The owner's servants came to him and said, 'Sir, didn't you sow good seed in your field? Where then did the weeds come from?' 'An enemy did this,' he replied. The servants asked him, 'Do you want us to go and pull them up?' 'No,' he answered, 'because while you are pulling the weeds, you may root up the wheat with them. Let both grow together until the harvest. At that time I will tell the harvesters: First collect the weeds and tie them in bundles to be burned; then gather the wheat and bring it into my barn.'"

What makes this parable so remarkable is that Jesus fully explains it. And until recently I hadn't connected the dots, even though verses 36-43 have been in my Bible for quite a long time: "Then he (Jesus) left the crowd and went into the house. His disciples came to him and said, 'Explain to us the parable of the weeds in the field.' He answered, 'The one who sowed the good seed is the Son of Man. The field is the world, and the good seed stands for the sons of the kingdom. The weeds are the sons of the evil one, and the enemy who sows them is the devil. The harvest is the end of the age, and the harvesters are angels. As the weeds are pulled up and burned in the fire, so it will be at the end of the age. The Son of Man will send out his angels, and they will weed out of his kingdom everything that causes sin and all who do evil. They will throw them into the fiery furnace, where there will be weeping and gnashing of teeth. Then the righteous will shine like the sun in the kingdom of their Father. He who has ears, let him hear."

This parable certainly seems to describe what we see happening all around us. The Church, at least in most of the Western world, has been asleep in many regards, and as a result the church and the world are nearly indistinguishable. At the end of the age, there will be two simultaneous gatherings, two "coming togethers." None of us in the Western World have ever lived outside of a denominational reality— the Church has been divided up into various denominations for our entire life experience. Yet those denominational lines are diminishing in importance rapidly. The world and its values, apart from biblical truth, are aligning forces; simultaneously, so is the Church, with a unity based on and growing out of the whole truth of God's Word. Denominational labels mean very little: you can find a Presbyterian church that has far more in common with an Assemblies of God church, than, say, two Baptist churches have with each other. And did you know that by statistical standards, we're either in the end of the age harvest or rapidly approaching it? More people around the globe have become Christians in the last 25 years than in the previous 2,000 years combined! At one point recently, "it was estimated that an average of nearly 300,000 people were coming to faith every day. In some nations, it was estimated that people were being born again at a faster rate than they were being born."[1] According to Jesus' parable in Matthew 13, what accompanies the great harvest at the end of the age? The gathering together—the unifying—of the body of Christ.

One of my volunteer jobs is to be the treasurer for my son's high school marching band booster club. It gives me a great chance to serve, but it also gives me an opportunity to intersect with the community instead of spending all my time with church folk. When I first took the position, I had to put an asterisk next to my offer, because it was right about the same time as I was concluding my time as pastor at Community of Hope. I wasn't sure what was next, or even where I might be in the future. We wanted to stay in Tucson, and I believed God was calling me to live out my life in Tucson, but I was unemployed. The other officers in the booster club knew this, so it was a natural question for them to ask, "So, do you have a job?" I thanked them for asking, and told them I did. I briefly described my job with 4Tucson, and one of them asked, "You mean your job is to help churches in Tucson work together?" I said "yes," and there was a long pause. You know what came next? A near revival right there in Starbucks. "Really? That's your job? That's the coolest thing I've ever heard." People who aren't even Christians are big fans of Christian unity. And when they see it actually happening at deeply significant levels rather than just described as a concept, look out!

---

1. Rick Joyner, The Harvest (New York: Simon & Schuster, 1999), p.8

Rick Joyner was given a vision of the days to come in 1987, published as *The Harvest.* He wrote, "For the coming harvest, the Lord is preparing a great spiritual 'fishnet' which will be able to hold the catch that is coming. This net is formed by the linking together of His people. The strength of this net will be determined by the strength of the interrelationships and intercommunication of His people...This is not only happening in the local churches among members, but between ministries, congregations, and the different streams in the body of Christ throughout cities, states, and crossing international barriers around the world. As this time unfolds, great and strong bonds will be formed between Christians all over the world until at the end, the unity of all Christians will be a reality. This will not be a unity of conformity, but a unity in diversity, because Christians will have matured and grown strong enough not to be threatened by others who are not exactly like them, but all will be seeking to grow up into Jesus...Some leaders will actually disband their organizations as they realize they are no longer relevant to what God is doing. Others will just leave them behind to disband themselves. Ultimately, all circles of ministry or influence with individual identities will dissolve into a single identity of simply being Christians for all who become part of this harvest. Individual units may form for strategic purposes such as a specific mission, or to reach a specific target group, city, or region, but distinctions will be based around function and purpose instead of differences in doctrine or procedure...Single presbyteries will form over cities and localities. These will be made up of pastors and leaders from many different denominations, movements and independent churches. Their unity in purpose, as well as that of the various congregations, will be a marvel to the world that is degenerating into chaos and paranoia...Those who enter into the unity of the true Spirit will not even be aware of it; their attention will not be on the church and what she is attaining but on the Lord Himself. The advancing church is soon to rise above worshiping the temple of the Lord to worshiping the Lord of the temple."

"For God knew His people in advance, and he chose them to become like His Son." (Romans 8:29 NLT) As we see the Son more clearly, we become gloriously blinded to the artificially erected barriers that have balkanized the body of Christ. God chose us to be like His Son, to be passionate about the things His Son is passionate about. We are called to

127

be an answer to Jesus' prayer, and to invest in His strategy for revealing His love and grace and truth to a watching and needy world.

Most of Section 2 has focused on relationships. Jesus' surprising strategy has little to do with structure, programs, or events, and everything to do with relationships that reflect and draw from the free-flowing love between Father and Son. Nevertheless, it can be very helpful to see how all of this manifests in a real city, in real time, with real people. That's the purpose of Section 3—to give a clear picture of how Jesus' surprising strategy is being revealed in one city: Tucson, Arizona.

PRACTICAL STEPS TO INVEST IN OUR COMMONWEALTH IN HEAVEN

1. Take some time to examine areas where you've allowed your experience to water down your understanding of God's promises rather than God's promises raising the level of expectation of your experience. Healing? Freedom? Prayer? How about in the area of unity, particularly comparing your expectations to John 17, 1 Corinthians 12, and Ephesians 4?

2. What are the strengths in your particular part of the body of Christ? What are the areas of the Christian life that are the least developed? Compare to Foster's list of the six streams of Christian tradition on page 119. What strategic connections could you make to parts of the body that excel where you and your congregation lag behind?

3. Whatever Bible reading program you're using, if you're not in God's Word on a consistent basis, please fix that today. Ask God to give you a John 17, 1 Corinthians 12 and Ephesians 4 lens as you read. Make note of all the new panoramas that open up when you shed the individualistic lens that's so counter to the biblical worldview. Make sure that your new parameters are wider than just your local congregation, and encompass at least your whole city or geographic area.

4. If you're part of a traditionally structured congregation (one that has

a staff of at least a pastor), examine the roles of the pastor and the roles of the congregation. Whose job is it to do ministry? The correct answer, according to the New Testament, is the congregation. The staff's job is to equip everybody else to do the ministry. Does your congregation operate that way? What would it mean if you did? If you're not part of the staff and wish your congregation did more to unite with other congregations, whose job is it to make that happen?

5. Try unity as a method of evangelism. Love and serve other Christians in public enough ways that others have a chance of noticing. Then see what happens.

6. If you're in a congregation, denomination, association, or any other group (large or small) that tends to emphasize your uniqueness at the expense of the unity and cohesion of the whole body of Christ, pray for a clearer picture of Jesus. Pray for a stronger connection to the Head of the body. Pray for the Lord's awesome character and power to be so evident that humility grows naturally. Pray for Jesus' love to so captivate your group that the sectarian attitudes don't have to be argued away, but simply melt away in His glorious presence.

SECTION THREE

MAKING
UNITY VISIBLE

ONE CITY'S STRATEGIES

Written collaboratively with Mark Harris,
founder and executive director of 4Tucson

In the first section we saw that if unity isn't a priority for us, we're out of line with the prayers of God's only Son. And the unity that Jesus prayed for and the New Testament describes is not just an internal unity within a local congregation. It's a visible, citywide unity, profound enough to catch the attention of a watching world. In the second section we saw that unity is primarily relational and always a work in progress, something that this side of heaven will be incomplete and partial. How we love one another, and how far we progress through the various levels of unity, will determine how much of Jesus' prayer gets answered in our city.

Now we're going to take an in depth look at how visible unity is beginning to manifest in one city—Tucson. 4Tucson is an organization based on Jesus' surprising strategy, with the goal of unifying and mobilizing the body of Christ in order to see our city transformed.

In February 2013, 30 Tucson churches began praying for a "church of the week" that has partnered with 4Tucson. One week it will be a Presbyterian church; the next week, a Nazarene church. Non-denominational, Lutheran, Covenant, Baptist, and many other flavors are in the lineup. Some are large, well-resourced suburban churches; others are small, under-funded urban churches. Still others are "house" churches, meeting in a coffee shop or a trailer park. Some are primarily Hispanic; others are predominantly African American or Anglo. Each week, those in attendance at participating congregations will hear a little about another church in the community, then join sisters and brothers around the city in praying for whatever requests that week's church submitted.

Thirty congregations is a nice start, but it's still less than 10 percent of the city's Christian congregations. Nobody turned us down when we launched it; but the program at first only hit the radar of primarily those whose pastors are experiencing growing levels of unity with one another. I dream of the day when praying for other congregations in Tucson will become standard operating procedure. I have this vision of a Tucson Christian visiting a friend's congregation and being shocked when they don't mention another church by name in their prayers.

When this vision becomes reality in Tucson, will we have arrived? Will our unity have met the visibility standards required by the control tower of John 17? Not even close. If 100 percent of churchgoers in Tucson not only prayed but practiced Christian unity in and between their congregations, do you know how visible that would make Christian unity in our city? I can tell you exactly—it would be 93 percent *in*visible. Only seven percent of Tucson's population is part of a Christian church on a given Sunday.

Starter questions

Every city in the world has problems. In America, the root of most of our cities' difficulties comes from well-intentioned people trying to do the right thing; making far reaching decisions that impact the entire city with no foundational principles or framework from which to work. Therefore, the actions they take are largely experiments with high hopes. Our decision makers are truly optimistic they will find solutions to help alleviate the pain and suffering they see in their communities.

As Christians, we believe God's Word serves as a time-tested framework from which we are able to evaluate our city's deepest problems, apply the principles we see from the Bible, and develop solutions that truly help people both in the short-term and long-term. Back up and park on that sentence for a second. Are we saying that pastors make the best economists, or that Bible students are automatically educational experts, or that church employees guarantee the success of your city's sports franchises? Hardly. Most Christians aren't professional Christians: their day job is outside of the church. They're "tentmakers," to use the term that shows up in the New Testament (Acts 18:3), people who are devoted followers of Christ but who make their living through so-called "secular" employment. In the process, they develop expertise in some aspect of culture while maintaining a biblical worldview and an ultimate allegiance to Christ. In that context, then, we can say that God intends to use His followers, working together like different parts of the same body, to implement biblical solutions that will benefit every citizen and ultimately bring glory to the name of Jesus.

It's important for every Christian to be able to answer two main questions with a resounding, "Yes!" If you're unable to answer these two questions affirmatively without hesitation, then there's a third question you should consider.

The first question is this: *Do I really love my city the way God loves my city?* In Luke 13:34, Jesus looked over the city of Jerusalem and said, "O Jerusalem, Jerusalem, you who kill the prophets and stone those sent to you, how often I have longed to gather your children together, as a hen gathers her chicks under her wings, but you were not willing!" When looking at your city, are you able to see what God sees? Does it break your heart when the citizens largely are not willing to follow God? Does it break your heart that your schools teach things that lead your children away from God? Does it break your heart to see a young mom take the life of her child through abortion? Does it break your heart to see families suffer from the ungodly choices they make? Do you get upset when you see graffiti; not because it looks bad, but because you see it as a symptom of a deeper problem: individuals who deface your city because they don't respect themselves or other people? When you contemplate these and many other symptoms, do you react like Christ reacted—not with judgment and criticism, but with compassion and healing? "Jesus went through all the towns and villages, teaching in their synagogues, preaching the good news of the kingdom and healing every disease and sickness. When he saw the crowds, he

135

had compassion on them, because they were harassed and helpless, like sheep without a shepherd." (Matthew 9:35-36) Do you have a heart for your city like God has a heart for the city?

The second question is this: ***Do I really love other followers of Jesus in my city?*** There are people throughout your city who believe God has called them to make a positive difference in their generation. They want to live out Matthew 5:16: "In the same way, let your light shine before others, so that they may see your good works and give glory to your Father who is in heaven." (ESV) These Christians have families, mortgages, cars that break down, leaky roofs, and health challenges that slow them down. Do you hurt when a fellow follower of Jesus hurts? Do you pray for the success of other believers? Do you desire to know their families and the personal struggles they face? Do you know where they are spiritually and pray about areas where they need to grow? Do you encourage them as they try to grow the Kingdom of God in your city? Do you love other follow-ers of Jesus, not only those who worship in a different manner or language than you, but also those whose areas of experience and ex-pertise differ from yours as well? Do you really love other followers of Jesus?

> **While the city's ills may not be your fault, they are your responsibility.**

If you're not able to definitively say you love your city and you love those who serve in His name, then you may want to ask yourself **a third question**: ***Am I willing to allow God to change my heart to love the things He loves?*** That's a dangerous prayer to pray. God *will* change your heart, because He loves you and He loves the people in your city.

Once love for your city, and love for the body of Christ in it, is firmly established, a change of perspective begins to grow. It's easy to notice the problems in your city. But if we regularly pray for the city, God will do the same thing He did when Jesus told His disciples to pray for the Lord of the harvest to send out workers into His harvest field: He'll send the ones praying! Luke 10:2 says, "The harvest is plentiful, but the workers are few. Ask the Lord of the harvest, therefore, to send out workers into his harvest field." What's the next word? "Go!" While the city's ills may not be your fault, as a follower of Christ you absolutely must come to the place that you realize this: the city's ills are your *responsibility*.

4TUCSON'S VISION AND MISSION

When 4Tucson started in 2009, we were unaware of other city models we could imitate. It could be that such ignorance was intentional on God's part, because models and strategies have to be birthed in prayer by people who love and are invested in their city. As we prayed for our city, a strategy began to unfold that was so big, so strategically and biblically sound, the only explanation had to be it was from God. Simultaneously, pastors were gathering together for the first time in any significant number to pray on a mountain overlooking Tucson for 72 hours. I believe that prayer summit changed the spiritual climate of the city and made the birth of 4Tucson possible.

4Tucson's vision is to "serve as a catalyst to engage the Christian community to bring about spiritual and societal transformation for the prosperity of the entire city." 4Tucson's mission is to "partner with every sector and domain of society based on common love, common goals, and the common good to make Tucson one of the most livable cities in the world, allowing each partner to determine the part it should play."

Both of those are lifelong, generational goals—far bigger than any one person's capacity to wrap his or her arms around. Yet one of the most comforting beliefs that sustain us through the many challenges is that this is God's idea, not ours. He's invited us to play a part in it, but if we choose to decline, it's still His vision and He'll find someone else to carry it out.

4TUCSON OPERATES WITH SEVEN FOUNDATIONAL PRINCIPLES

1. **Centered unapologetically on Jesus. (John 14:6)** As we saw back in Chapter 1, unity and truth are partners, not enemies. The way to achieve unity and blessing in the city is not to try to hide Jesus in the corner as if we're embarrassed by Him.

137

2. **Church based.** (Matthew 16:18) God's design is for the local church to lead the way to lasting solutions for the ills of every society. 4Tucson is not a church, so when people seek to join us, one of our requirements is that they be involved in, or become part of, a local congregation where principles of unity are learned at highly relational levels.

3. **Community focused.** (Jeremiah 29:7) It's easy for churches to become inwardly focused. To be community focused requires constant intentionality. As we pray for and serve our city and see it begin to prosper, God's peace and prosperity is like a rising tide that raises the level of every boat on the water. Everyone in the community is a beneficiary of those who obey God's mandate to pray for and serve our city.

4. **Collaborative approach.** (Ephesians 4:11-16) We are better together! Every part of the body is important. We each hold a piece of the puzzle to our community's needs. We need each other to present a balanced picture of Jesus to the world.

5. **Christ-like in word and deed.** (Colossians 3:17) In all we do for others, we should do it in the name and manner of Jesus. Jesus is our motivation, our source of strength, and our example for interacting with our community.

6. **Citywide, strategic prayer.** (John 14:13-14) Could it be that the pathologies of each city are there because we don't ask God for His solutions and do something different? Could it be we really don't believe God will make a difference if we just asked Him? We have determined to ask and to seek God in prayer together, not just individually.

7. **Cultural transformation.** (Luke 19:41-42) God revealed to His followers the things that make for peace in every city. When we follow His leadership, we will see evidence of His activity and the result will be peace.

4TUCSON'S CORE VALUES

The first thing to notice about these core values is they have far more to do with relationships and character than to do with activity. I'm convinced activity has a way of generating itself, sometimes seemingly without human intervention. Certainly, we'll have to act on our values: visibility requires action. Yet activity isn't the place to start, because unless it's built on a solid foundation, activity will collapse when the rains fall and the wind blows. (Matthew 7:27) Like the graphic indicates, we're sure there's more to the whole picture than God has presently revealed. But we're also quite convinced God has given us several key pieces to the puzzle.

Unity. "May they be brought to complete unity to let the world know that you sent me and have loved them even as you have loved me." (John 17:23) As He headed to the cross, Jesus focused His prayers on the unity of His followers as a means for letting the world know the love that characterizes God. If it was such a high priority for Jesus, surely it needs to be a high priority of ours, too. The unity Jesus prayed for was a visible unity that the world would be able to notice.

Collaboration. "Plans fail for lack of counsel, but with many advisers they succeed." (Proverbs 15:22) Tucsonans live in a country, state, and city deeply characterized by a spirit of independence. While an independent spirit has assets, it also has liabilities. It's time for Christians to lead the way in changing the question to, "How can we go farther together?"

Integrity. "You are the salt of the earth. But if the salt loses its saltiness, how can it be made salty again? It is no longer good for anything, except to be thrown out and trampled by men." (Matthew 5:13) When the church starts to reflect the world instead of shape it, we have a big problem. Part of 4Tucson's commitment to integrity is an accountability pledge in our code of ethics: "I will conduct my personal and public life according to the standards taught in the Bible, and agree to be accountable to other members of 4Tucson."

Service. "Now that I, your Lord and Teacher, have washed your feet, you also should wash one another's feet. I have set you an example that you should do as I have done for you." (John 13:14-15) Service is the sweet spot the whole world understands. When Christ-followers enter into their spheres of influence with the question, "How can I serve?" relationships are built and doors often open for the sharing of the Gospel of Jesus Christ.

DOMAIN STRATEGY

In November 2012, I attended Movement Day in New York City, a grassroots gathering of leaders from 300 city transformation movements around the country and globe. One of the most encouraging aspects to the conference was seeing how God was downloading a similar vision everywhere—a vision people weren't copying or learning from one another, but simultaneously receiving from God directly.

The Bible teaches God has given us responsibility over His creation: "You gave them charge of everything You made, putting all things under their authority." (Psalm 8:6 NLT) Every domain of society will be given to believers and every domain will serve and obey God: "And the kingdom and the dominion and the greatness of the kingdoms under the whole heaven shall be given to the people of the saints of the Most High; his kingdom shall be an everlasting kingdom, and all dominions shall serve and obey him." (Daniel 7:27 ESV)

Every city has three primary sectors in which it is organized: the Public Sector, the Private Sector, and the Social Sector.

The **Public Sector** is owned by the state and exists to provide services in the public interest like police and fire services, education, clean water, and waste management. The **Private Sector** includes companies, corporations, small businesses, and private banks which are not controlled by the state but are privately owned and profit motivated. The **Social Sector** includes voluntary, religious and not-for-profit activities which may include the arts, charities, education, politics, religion, research, and other endeavors. Although not an agency of the state, a non-profit may have to meet state requirements to secure or maintain its charitable status.

Within the three sectors of society, 4Tucson identified 12 "domains" or spheres of activity in the community in which influence is exercised. The Domain Wheel for 4Tucson isn't identical to that for other cities, but the concept behind it is. There could be many more domains in Tucson, but to keep it manageable, we started with a dozen. The domains most influential in Tucson are Business, Education, Health Care, Justice, Church, Prayer, Sports, Environment, Social Services, Philanthropy, Government, and Media/Arts.

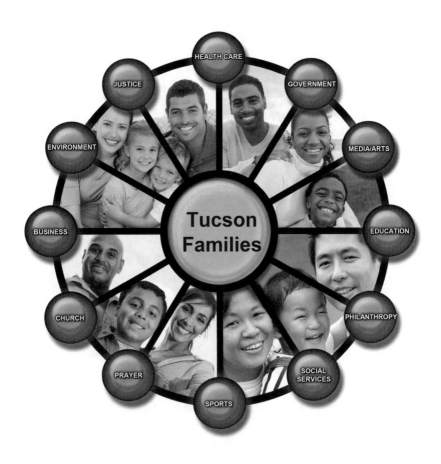

The domains work together to support and build up Tucson families. The family is the smallest unit that God created for the development of a healthy society. All the domains exist to serve families by providing jobs, products and services, health care, education, and so on, to help families thrive. This is vital—since the family is an earthly picture of the heavenly reality of a triune God. It's where we learn to love, to give, to serve and receive, to forgive, to think, to make wise, healthy choices: in short, to reflect the very nature of God in the world.

While a family can certainly contain a single parent or unmarried person, God's pattern for marriage between a man and woman is clear. Even more, when couples follow His teachings for married relationships in the Bible (Ephesians 5:21-6:4 and Colossians 3:15-21 are just two passages), there are many benefits to the couple as well as to society as a whole. In his book, *The Marriage Problem: How Our Culture Has Weakened Families*, Dr. James Wilson says married people "are happier than unmarried ones of the same age, not only in the United States, but in at least 17 other countries where similar inquiries have been made. And there seems to be good reasons for that happiness. People who are married not only have higher incomes and enjoy greater emotional support, they tend to be healthier." Healthy marriages produce healthier, happier employers and employees. They produce healthier, happier children. Healthy and happy people make wiser life choices. In the 4Tucson model, everything in society revolves around and serves the needs of the family. What a culture believes and practices concerning the family directly impacts its citizens and the city's health and well-being.

> Only the whole body of Christ can address the big picture problems for the whole city.

One of the absolute keys to the effectiveness of the domain structure is that each would have a domain leader who would work to identify and enlist other Christians who have an interest in working within that particular domain. The domain leader needs to be someone with expertise in their particular domain, but also an understanding and support for the whole picture. The domain leader also needs to be respected in the community as a bridge builder with integrity, and must have enough time available to build relationships and grow the domain.

In order for each domain to begin exercising godly influence, a structure is needed that would make it possible for interested Christians from diverse spiritual backgrounds to meet other Christians they would not encounter otherwise. Only the whole body of Christ can address the big picture problems for the whole city. Once relationships develop, it's possible to begin identifying problems within the domain, compare ideas and create biblical solutions. We identified four areas of focus for each domain leader to begin the task of assembling his or her team.

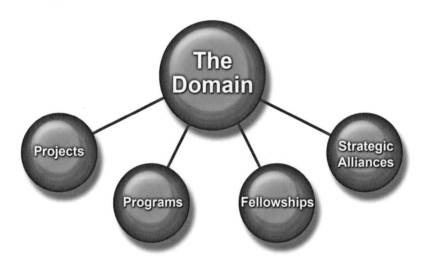

Programs are sustainable, ongoing training and ministry development opportunities designed to equip those who want to become more influential within the community. For instance, Patriot Academy gives students an understanding not only of our political system but the godly heritage of our country, training up educated citizens and raising up future political leaders. (See next chapter for some details of this program.)

Projects are activities that provide opportunities for believers to work with other individuals or groups in order to make the city a better place to live. Christians can partner with local public schools to love, provide for, mentor, serve, and tutor children. One of our favorite sayings is, "You don't have to believe like I believe to care about what I care about."

Fellowships are regular gatherings designed to promote Christian unity and prayer within the domain. As relationships grow, all kinds of partnerships develop that are organized at grassroots levels, without requiring additional oversight or organizational energy. In Tucson, pastors and ministry leaders meet monthly to address the question, "How is the body of Christ in our city responding to a particular area of need?" The times of fellowship and prayer in table groups are as important as the presentations on the topic.

Strategic alliances are partnerships with other Christian organizations, using our combined resources, programs, and expertise to touch the city and increase the impact of both groups. Every ministry in the city has a piece of the puzzle. Only by strategically aligning and helping one another does the picture of God's favored future for the city begin to come into focus. All the common cause ministries mentioned in Chapter 5 need to strategically align with one another and with the churches in order for their efforts to enhance and not detract from one another.

DON'T DESALINATE!

Jesus says to all of His followers, past, present, and future, "You are the salt of the earth." (Matthew 5:13) As Reggie McNeal taught at the 2012 annual gathering of Lutheran Congregations in Mission for Christ, "the Church is often guilty of becoming a desalinization plant—sucking the salt out of the world." If ministry is understood primarily as what happens within the walls of the church (either literal or organizational walls), it's inevitable we'll undercut and destroy Jesus' salty declaration. Yet for most of the last 1,700 years, that's exactly what's happened, creating a caste system within Christianity. First class Christians go to seminary, forego working in the sinful world, and find a job in the church. Second class Christians suffer through their day jobs but then serve the Lord in the voluntary work they do for the church during evenings and weekends. The Church celebrates when a young adult is deeply touched by God and trades in his or her "secular" work for a more holy profession within the confines of the church. Some traditions even use the word "call" as a way of distinguishing and elevating church employment over and above secular employment. This is tragically sad and incalculably devastating.

Salt confined to the salt shaker flavors nothing. Jesus added, "Neither do people light a lamp and put it under a bowl" (Matthew 5:15), yet that's exactly what we have done. We try to gather up as many of the light rays as possible and collect them under a bowl with a steeple on top of it. Countless Christian business leaders, educators, government employees, and doctors feel guilty they don't have more time to give to the "church" when, in fact, that's exactly opposite of the proper perspective. The church needs to empower and encourage them to be salt and light right where they are. That's the only way our culture changes. Christian athletes have in recent years attempted to find ways to use their day jobs to shine the light brighter, but it's so foreign to our way of thinking that one athlete's efforts in this regard were actually copyrighted: "Tebowing."

The domain structure, fully implemented, has much potential to reverse this devastating phenomenon.

Funding

How does 4Tucson pay for all of this? That thoroughly practical question actually prevented the vision from really taking off for a few years. Lots of people around the city were excited as the vision was initially presented; I was one of those. Yet at the time I was invested full-time in leading a local congregation and had very little extra time available. My church had graciously reworked my job description so that some of the community work I was doing was seen as *part* of my responsibility, not moonlighting. Even so, when push came to shove, it was clear what had to wait until the next day or week. Clarity on our ministry assignments is crucial: nobody wins if time spent on a citywide organization actually ends up being time subtracted from tending to the health of the local churches.

The key decision that caused 4Tucson to advance and grow was to invite domain leaders to see themselves as missionaries to Tucson, which includes every missionary's favorite responsibility—raising their own monetary support. As of this writing, 4Tucson has domain leaders in nine of the 12 domains. All are either at a place in life where they can volunteer their time or are willing to raise

> People invest in the things they care about, and care more about the things they invest in.

whatever funds are needed. In my case, I'm the primary (and at the time I started, only) breadwinner for my family of six.

Having domain leaders responsible for raising their own support accomplishes several things. It weeds out the faint of heart. It ensures the people leading the domain are networkers, absolutely vital for the success of the endeavor. And it provides people a meaningful opportunity to invest in the work of the domain in a deeply personal way. It's also the only way to get the ball rolling. For individuals to support the vision, they have to hear about it and see the progress. That can only happen with some leaders fully invested on the front end.

The second key component to 4Tucson's funding strategy is to invite individuals and organizations to each invest a little as well. Staff raising their own support is an ideal way to jump-start the process, but less effective as an ongoing strategy. Tucson isn't known for its philanthropic foundations with deep pockets. 4Tucson recognizes its need to grow a large base of support, not only because no other financial alternatives exist, but also because true unity requires everyone's engagement. Jesus said, "Where your treasure is, there your heart will be also." (Matthew 6:21) This statement isn't as much a command as it is simply a fact. People invest in the things they care about, and they care more about the things they invest in. If we want people to invest in Christian unity in our city and not merely be a fan of it, money is part of the equation. This remains one of our most significant challenges, perhaps illustrating a reason why Jesus spent more time teaching about money and possessions than He did about prayer or worship.

4Tucson invites individuals to partner for $10 a month. Very few people will actually find this taxing if the vision is made real enough. People are also told not to reduce their tithe to their church by this amount: as Bill Hybels is well known for saying, "The local church is the hope of the world." It would be counterproductive in the highest order for support to come at the expense of the local church. 4Tucson invites churches and organizations to partner at $35 a month. Of the first three churches to officially partner with us, one was a house church of 12 people, the other one of the largest congregations in the city. Both came in as equal partners. For both the individual and group partnerships, the amount is more of a principle than a fee, so variances can always be made. As the number of partners grow, the picture of the body of Christ in the city truly functioning as one body becomes clearer. At 4Tucson's website, you'll see churches from all over the metro area of all sizes, shapes, and colors—all committed to a common cause and all functioning as part of the answer to Jesus' powerful John 17 prayer.

Code of Ethics

When people partner with 4Tucson, they are asked to then agree to a Code of Ethics: "I pledge that, to the best of my ability, I will promote the unity of believers and actively work with other believers on projects, programs, and fellowships. If I do not already belong to a local church, I will make it a priority to join and support one. I will conduct my personal and public life according to the standards taught in the Bible, and agree to be accountable to other members of 4Tucson." This is provided on a business card that people can take with them wherever they go.

The first sentence of the code is an invitation to get involved. Promoting the unity of believers starts with a unilateral cease-fire agreement: no more badmouthing the church of a different flavor down the street. Feet don't have to become hands, but they certainly need to learn to love, appreciate, and support them. Like all biblical commands, it isn't only a prohibition of something *not* to do, but a mandate of something *to* do. The promise involves investing some time in citywide ventures, but it also means carrying out the activities that you might already be involved in from a new citywide, collaborative approach. "How can we do this together" is becoming the new question of choice in our city.

The second sentence of the code is going to become part of the solution to the shocking reality that 70 percent of Tucsonans claim to be Christian but only seven percent are actively connected to a local church. It's actually easy to meet people who get excited about this citywide vision and want to join 4Tucson. Yet when asked what church they're connected to, the answer is often, "None." A commitment to joining a local church must be a priority. Unity is primarily relational, and none of the levels of unity described in the previous section can be lived out in isolation. The "private religion" mantra in our country is totally foreign to the New Testament.

The last sentence of the code is a commitment to integrity. While no one in 4Tucson intends to legislate what accountability looks like, signing such a code will open up the doors for Christians in the city to begin to practice Level 5 unity, speaking the truth in love to one another, and creating a more humble and mature band of Christ-followers. It's also how integrity can begin to extend beyond church fellowships and out into the world of education, business, government—all the areas covered in the 12 domains.

Once someone agrees to the Code of Ethics, they're invited to pick a domain and jump in. Many initially have interest in multiple domains, but the volume of communication and activity in each can be overwhelming unless people narrow their focus. A person's ability to make a significant impact in their area of expertise also requires a focused approach to building relationships and collaboration. It's time to put the salt back in the vast ocean of our cities.

This chapter has largely dealt with the theory and rationale for 4Tucson's strategies. The fun comes in seeing those strategies in practice and celebrating the tangible results of visible unity. For a few of one city's stories, turn to the next and final chapter.

Chapter Eleven

One City's Stories

Written collaboratively with the 4Tucson team

Unity taps into the rivers of heaven. Phrased another way, love between brothers and sisters in Christ here on earth opens up avenues for love to flow between heaven and earth. We hear from God and receive from God in fresh ways when we are experiencing deepening levels of unity in fulfillment of Jesus' surprising strategy.

Before we share some actual stories of visible unity, let's look to the Scriptures one more time to discover God's intentions. "His story" is the best evaluator of history, always, even as it's being made.

John 17, 1 Corinthians 12, and Ephesians 4 are the trinity of "unity chapters" from the New Testament. In the Old Testament, rather than three chapters, we find three verses, all from the same chapter, Psalm 133. "How good and pleasant it is when brothers live together in unity! It is like precious oil poured on the head, running down on the beard, running down on Aaron's beard, down upon the collar of his robes. It is as if the dew of Hermon were falling on Mount Zion. For there the Lord bestows his blessing, even life forevermore."

Anyone who's been a fan of unity for any length of time is probably familiar with this psalm. Its brevity only adds to its beauty. There's always a tradeoff in choosing between English translations: this one (NIV 1984) keeps the intimate and familial language of "brothers" in verse one, but loses the inclusive language that ensures that the "sisters" see themselves as included from the beginning also. That is an English problem, not a Hebrew or Greek problem. The bigger translation issue, though, is not one of language but of cultures. Oil poured on my head, running down my face and staining my clothing, strikes me as something less than a blessing. Verse one is straightforward enough, but my choice of imagery to illustrate its blessing would probably involve my University of Arizona basketball team exorcising the Sun Devils 100 miles to the north. I can more easily get excited by sports victories than flowing oil and morning dew.

Instead of analyzing the details of the two images in verses two and three, look instead at the big picture. Both oil and water throughout the Scriptures are symbols of the Holy Spirit. Where unity prevails, the Holy Spirit moves. Another biblical symbol of the Holy Spirit is a dove, a gentle and easily disturbed bird. Discord and strife cause the Dove to fly elsewhere. But when love between sisters and brothers of Christ is flowing freely and uninhibited, the river of the Holy Spirit is, too. The blessings of the Holy Spirit flow from heaven, creating life abundant that begins now and is brought to perfection in the life to come.

We see this same reality in the New Testament. You'll recall the disciples had a lot of unifying and reconciling to do with one another as they obediently waited for the Holy Spirit to be poured out. Acts 1:14 gives us a very brief synopsis of the hard work being done: "They all joined together constantly in prayer, along with the women and Mary the mother of Jesus, and with his brothers." I have no doubt that the uncommon combination of grace and truth were put into practice repeatedly, with humility the sweet aroma of the room. Reconciliation doesn't happen any other way. And this work is what made it possible for the Holy Spirit to be poured out at Pentecost. Unity taps in to the rivers of heaven.

I've mentioned our congregation's 2007 mission trip to Tanzania already, as it was obviously a high impact chapter of my life. The unifying work done on the trip wasn't reconciling differences—it was overcoming ignorance. As an American Christian, I'd been ignorant of Third World Christianity. Ignorance is not bliss, and this lack of relationship on my part came with a great cost. When I returned, the first sermon series I preached was called, "From Tanzania to Tucson," and its purpose was to share vital lessons learned overseas and how we could apply them to the mission fields all around us in our own city. Little did I know at the time that one of the key epiphanies of that trip would also directly impact my work with 4Tucson in years to come. Part of our trip involved a couple of days at the Lutheran Bible Institute in the little village of Kiomboi in the middle of the country. One of the

> **If you want to go fast, go alone. If you want to go far, go together.**

first people I met, and the main person I remember, was a teacher there by the name of Mr. Mangi, a man small in stature but great in impact. He was one of the three people I most hoped to reconnect with in my return trip in 2009, a gift God graciously granted me. Mr. Mangi is an ever-flowing river of wisdom; I wrote down many of the things he said in my journal. But the one I now share every time I introduce 4Tucson to groups is this:

"If you want to go fast, go alone. But if you want to go far, go together."

HEAVENLY STAFF MEETINGS

One of the keys to Tucson becoming a visible answer to Jesus' John 17 prayer, I'm convinced, has become our weekly staff meeting. I realize "answer to prayer" and "staff meeting" rarely belong in the same sentence, so allow me to explain. I don't make such a claim because of the brilliance each of us brings to the table. We regularly comment that we don't know what we're doing, even though we *do* know Who we're following. And my claim isn't because it's always smooth sailing. The engineer in me likes to know where we are, where we're going, and exactly how we plan to get there. The engineer in me is usually disappointed. Our favorite analogy is that we're building this plane while we're flying it.

What makes the staff meetings heavenly is that it's a slice of unity so rarely tasted. I don't think any two of us come from the same denomination or stream of Christianity—but that's a bonus, not the core of what I'm addressing here. What I've never experienced before is an intentional and regular meeting of Christians who are each passionate about a different domain of society. Three of us—4Tucson directors for the education, prayer, and church domains—have been on the same team now for over 18 months. Six more have joined at various points during the last year. We've added in support staff (a director of membership services) and, of course, are led by our executive director and founder Mark Harris. The energy in the room is palpable, week after week. Each of us writes and emails one another a weekly report of what's been happening and what we're working on. The frustration we experience in our staff meetings is almost always a lack of time to share as many stories as we'd like of God at work in our city. That's a *wonderful* frustration to have!

I was so struck a while ago by the breadth and diversity of what God was doing, I jotted down the different topics raised as we went around the room. Here's a snapshot of one moment in time from one of our staff meetings:

- The government and education domains are working together to bring the Patriot Academy to Tucson to students. The Patriot Academy is a six-day political training and leadership program where students age 16-25 learn about America's system of government from a biblical worldview. The only other place this has been offered is in Texas.

- The social services domain is working with the church, business, and education domains to start a program called Neighborhood Totes, providing a weekend backpack filled with food for schoolchildren who rely on free meals during the week.

- The philanthropic domain is creating a series of elegant social events allowing people to hear the stories of what God is doing in our city and an opportunity to fund them.

- The church domain is working on a community Easter Sunrise service. Many churches don't offer sunrise services, and a few others did but decided this would be an opportunity to worship together as a citywide church. Most exciting is that one ethnic group has a longstanding tradition of offering their own Easter Sunrise service, and now is interested in partnering with the rest of the Christian community.

- The church and education domains gave a progress report on an upcoming Church School Partnership Workshop with 34 participating congregations. The city's largest school district, Tucson Unified School District (TUSD), not only enthusiastically endorses the concept, but is participating in the training both as presenters and recipients.

- The prayer domain director shared a couple of stories of city transformation conversations taking place in public places like In-N-Out Burger and Starbucks. In one instance, an administrator from TUSD overheard two people talking about city transformation and went over and asked them if they'd heard of 4Tucson. He'd learned about 4Tucson because of the work that the church and prayer domains had been doing in serving his school district. The two people he overheard turned out to be youth pastors—both of whom were already full partners with 4Tucson.

- The media and arts domain director reported on collaboration beginning among Christians within Tucson's diverse arts community.

- One of our success stories from 2012 was working with the government and business domains to create a public-private partnership that reopened several of the public swimming pools that had been closed due to budget cuts. My 4Tucson presentations around town always start with several of the statistics revealing the desperate need for transformation in our city. One of those needs shows up in the glaring lack of collaboration between branches of government, the public and private sectors, and so forth. I mentioned the closed pools in several of those presentations, since business leaders had offered a year earlier to partner to open the pools, but nothing ever came from their offer. One person heard that story, came up to me afterward and said, "I can fix that," and because of the relationships he had with all the key leaders, got the same proposal passed unanimously that had died in committee the year before. That one simple partnership made Tucson a more family-friendly city in 2012 than it had been in 2011. In this staff meeting, the government domain director reported that a city council member initiated conversation asking if we could help lead this effort again in 2013.

- The government, prayer, and church domains talked about several National Day of Prayer projects that will incorporate the entire community for the annual observance.

- The business domain had been one of the four lacking a director. Despite the absence of a staff-level leader, several people have worked together to create a monthly business fellowship as well as sponsor a few business domain projects. A guest to the staff meeting, interested in the business domain, offered to contact Christian business owners around town and share the vision with them. Since that morning, he and another man have agreed to join the team as co-business domain directors.

Not bad for a morning's work.

OCCUPYING THE TERRITORY

A statewide organization, BridgeBuilders International, has hosted an annual prophetic conference called Start the Year Right. In 2013, they invited 4Tucson to partner with them. One of the speakers was Lance Wallnau, author of *The 7 Mountain Mandate*, the seven mountains being spheres or domains of influence that must be captured if transformation is to affect an entire region or culture. Referencing Jesus' teaching in Matthew 12:43-45, Wallnau shared how our prayers for nationwide revival have hit the mark, but we've been too focused on instant gratification to notice. If God had answered all our prayers, he said, the cleansing of our nation would have been lost because we have to be prepared to occupy the territory we take. If we got what we wanted but didn't know what to do with it when we got it, we would actually be worse off than before. Germany in the 1930's is a case study in this truth.

The domain structure is a revelation from God for our day—and is the way to occupy territory in a way that blesses all the inhabitants. It's not a hostile takeover, but a "how can we serve and how can we help" means of blessing and influencing a domain. *Every* domain needs to be so influenced. This concept is not original to us in 4Tucson; Mark was introduced to the concept of domains of society by Pastor Bob Roberts of Northwood Baptist Church in Dallas, Texas, who had organized his congregation's mission work in Vietnam around domains. Part of the proof it's a revelation from God is that it's not entirely original to anyone. God certainly revealed these principles to some earlier than to others, and many have learned from others along the way. But in instance after instance and city after city, the concept has been born more out of prayer than out of studying someone else's work.

> Isn't it amazing how much you can accomplish if you don't care who gets the credit?

"FOLLOWING GOD AROUND TOWN AND TAKING NOTES"

That's how I've described my job at 4Tucson these last 20 months. Everyone is passionate about something, and 4Tucson's role is often little more than networking—introducing people to one another that might not have met otherwise. My pastor while I was in college had a plaque that said, "Isn't it amazing how much you can accomplish if you don't care who gets the credit?" It's easy to give away credit...and exceedingly wise. The more you praise others for their contributions, the more bridges get built. And, ultimately, so much is being accomplished that it isn't even tempting to take credit ourselves: the thought would be ridiculous even to our sinful selves! It's obviously God's handiwork.

A couple months ago I got a call from a director of the Navigators campus ministry at the University of Arizona. He had a group of about 100 students who wanted to go on a mission trip over spring break—to our very own city of Tucson! Can you hear the angels rejoicing? When a mission trip to your own city, at a fraction of the cost of going overseas, is as exciting as flying halfway around the world, that's obviously God at work. I contacted a couple of inner city churches that might have repair or remodeling needs. I mentioned Tucson Refugee Ministry to him, since there are thousands of refugees in Tucson, as well as got him connected with the ministry working to stop human trafficking in town. Additionally, the church-school partnerships springing up around town have resulted in a project of re-striping several of the outdoor courts for the public schools. That project is coordinated by a staff member from Community Renewal, another organization working for city transformation in Tucson.[1] All of these projects together combine to make a rich mission trip experience for the students, with the added benefit of being able to continue the work after spring break is over. Everyone wins when God is in the driver's seat and we're paying attention.

More like spaghetti than meatballs

The domain structure functions as an intentional catalyst, identifying areas where God's people can connect and start working together. But the work rarely falls into isolated, tightly compacted units. It's more like spaghetti, all over the place and interconnected, than it is like meatballs. All the domains intersect, and it's often in those intersections where the most exciting activity takes place. Some structure is essential, but since unity is inherently relational, the goal is to follow the relationships rather than compartmentalize into nice but rigid boxes. For example, since the prayer domain director is the one with the most connections among youth pastors, he's the one to organize the fellowship of youth pastors, even though it fits into the church domain box.

Here are several examples of spaghetti around Tucson supplied by the 4Tucson staff team:

1. Community Renewal is a partner in several citywide transformation ministries, and in particular does amazing work among several marginalized parts of our community. See www.transformingtucson.org for more information.

158

REMEMBERING THE CITY'S CHRISTIAN HERITAGE

We're working with a variety of Christian artists, musicians, historians, pastors, and business leaders in an effort to develop a project we are calling City Psalms—a collaborative multimedia venture we hope will be a unifying resource for our Christian community and a platform to lead us into a common vision for Tucson. Our vision is to help reestablish our Christian heritage in Tucson by telling stories of God's goodness from Tucson's history and reengage Christians into God's vision for our city by creating media resources such as music, art, books, curriculum, web pages, and film. Hidden in the day-to-day fabric of our community are incredible stories of how God has used His people to bring His leadership into our community. We want to bring those stories to the forefront and empower believers to pray into how God wants to lead us, collectively, in the future.

DOWNTOWN PRAYER WALKING

For nearly one year, up to a dozen pastors from congregations all across Tucson met together weekly to "prayer walk" the streets of downtown. Within that year of prayer walking, we were able to witness God move in incredible ways, including the planting of five churches in the downtown area.

PUBLIC SCHOOL PRAYER VIGILS

A highly anointed young adult, Matt Merrill is one of the founders of Eleven11, a ministry bringing prayer back into the public schools in an incredibly creative and effective way. (Eleven11 is one of the ministries of BridgeBuilders International). Matt and his team organize 24 hour prayer vigils in the auditoriums of public high schools around the state. They pay the full price for rental, security, and insurance, eliminating the first round of potential objections. Then they invite Christians they know from among the student body, faculty, or staff, as well as churches, particularly those from surrounding neighborhoods. Those prayer vigils have created some amazing testimonies, including lives literally being saved as students contemplating suicide found their way into the auditoriums. From 4Tucson's perspective, even though we had nothing to do with getting this ministry started, the church, education, and prayer domains all want to partner with them and fan the flames already burning. Coincidentally, church, education, and prayer are the three domains that have had staff attention in 4Tucson for the longest, so we've had the most time to build our networks. The church school partnership workshop grew directly out of the relationships built around the city.

INTERSECTIONS OF FAITH AND LEARNING

An English teacher attended a monthly fellowship of Christian educators. As a result of the encouragement and some of the training the education domain provided on Religious Freedom day, she incorporated the President's Proclamation into a reading assignment for her middle school students and also shared the origin of Dr. Martin Luther King's beliefs: the Bible. Prior to this lesson, she had described feeling discouraged that her teaching was useless. Now she is excited about other intersections of faith and learning, and the opportunity to legally and appropriately integrate the Bible and Christianity into the curriculum.

REASON FOR THE SEASON

One elementary school family here in Tucson purchased Gateways to Better Education's Christmas card and with two other families hand delivered them to every teacher, office staff, and principal at their school. Each card helps restore the true meaning of Christmas by telling a humorous story that includes legal documentation and suggested lesson plans. One teacher said, "I felt so strong in what I was doing this year. When I would doubt, I would take out the card and say, 'No, No, I can do this!'" The principal stated the card opened his eyes to things he did not know. Then he proceeded to share things he would do differently next year. This was an easy, non-threatening, effective way to begin to change the culture and atmosphere of a whole school.

HOLIDAY FAMILY HAVEN

4Tucson teamed with a local church to sponsor families at schools in the neighborhood around the church for the Christmas holidays.

The project, called "Neighborhood Haven," collected turkeys and other food and provided two Christmas gifts for each child in a sponsored family. Families shared their stories and how much the food and gifts meant to them; several cried and prayed with us. The Neighborhood Totes project (mentioned earlier in this chapter) grew out of the incredible impact from this simple partnership.

ALL IN 60 MINUTES

I attended a large citywide Multicultural Pastors' Christmas party. It used to be a party of the Hispanic Pastors' Association, but as a result of the relationships built over the last year, they wanted to invite the rest of the city pastors and changed the name. I "just happened" to be sitting next to a pastor of a church I'd only recently met, and he told me about an upcoming meeting two days later with City of South Tucson officials regarding zoning for a new 12-unit recovery center the congregation wanted to open. I asked if I could come and lend some support. It was an amazing collaborative effort of the church, business, government, and social services domains, though 4Tucson had nothing to do with any of it. The owner of the unit is working with the congregation to have them eventually own the facility. The government officials want it to happen, and a police officer present gave his cell number to the pastor so that they can work directly together, encouraging him to call whenever there were incidents in the ministry, and together they'd decide whether an arrest would be the most helpful way to handle the situation. The zoning administrator, business license manager, and city manager all dropped by to give their approval to the project. The whole process took an hour. I felt privileged just to watch and observe God at work.

FREE PATRIOT

The government domain director traveled to Phoenix to meet with a state senator about the Patriot Academy, sharing how they'd need a major portion of the State Capitol buildings for the program. The meeting ran long, but through a series of "coincidences" they ended up meeting the woman in charge of operations of the House and Senate

161

building, who in turn put the Patriot Academy on the calendar and offered the entire building for our use—at no charge.

THE PARABLE OF THE CHAIRS

A pastor of one of the new downtown area churches was moving into new facilities, yet really wanted to attend the Church School Partnership Workshop even though things weren't entirely ready for that evening's service. He strongly sensed God telling him to attend the training and not worry about the upcoming service. At the training, another pastor from across town came over and asked him how he was doing. He shared that his most immediate need was that he still didn't have chairs—for that evening's service! This pastor had some in storage and offered to give him the chairs on the spot.

Even though I have the high honor and privilege of waking up every day wondering how I can align myself most effectively that day with Jesus' prayer strategy in John 17, I remain awestruck that *this* would be the focal point of Jesus' prayer life at the moment of truth.

"May they be brought to complete unity to let the world know…"

PRACTICAL LESSONS LEARNED (OR STILL BEING LEARNED) THROUGH 4TUCSON

1. **Communication is the most complicated part of the whole process.** Every congregation develops its own culture. Add in denominational protocols, ethnic distinctives, generational preferences, and personality differences—and communication is a logistical nightmare. Unity has to develop into Level 5, where people speak the truth in love to one another, apologize, and forgive, then do it regularly and consistently. There's no possible way communication will happen perfectly and without offense.

2. **Until congregations view citywide unity as a mandate, progress will be limited.** The volume of communication necessary

to unite and mobilize Christians in every domain is staggering, and much of it has to flow through the churches. The job descriptions of most church staff require them to be focused on what's happening in and through the congregation. Citywide progress is seen as an extra if we have time, meaning that emails and phone calls can get delayed or ignored with the best of intentions to get around to them later. We haven't figured out yet how to solve this issue. Even city-minded pastors and city-minded congregations are battling a congregationally-focused culture. The best solution we've come up with so far is for a congregation to appoint and empower one person, staff or otherwise, for whom receiving and forwarding communication is at or near the top of the list of his or her priorities. That person eagerly anticipates learning what opportunities are out there in the city, and then is expected to pass that information along in appropriate ways within the congregation.

3. **Relational capital is a very powerful thing.** It isn't possible to build relationships with everyone, but if we both know and trust the same person, there can be a godly transference—and what would have taken years can happen in moments.

4. **That same transference works negatively, too.** When trust is broken, the negative ripples are even more present than the positive ones. Integrity can't possibly be overstated. Caution needs to be exercised in allowing people into positions of significant influence when their spiritual maturity or character hasn't already been tested and proven strong.

5. **As people get excited about working together, there's still a daily dying to self that's essential.** Everyone has to come into every context asking the question, "How can I submit to others? Serve others? Love others? Celebrate others' ideas?" as opposed to "How can I lobby for my perspective?" "How can I recruit others to support my idea?" "How can I argue persuasively for my vantage point?"

6. **Yet at the same time, every part of the body does have strengths—unique strengths, unique perspectives.** That means the goal is to get to a place where everyone wants to share freely their input, and where everyone *wants* everyone to share their perspective. Submission to others doesn't mean becoming wallflowers, hiding our lamps under bushels. Our ongoing African-American/Anglo pastors' political discussions are venturing into these waters right now. We're just starting the same thing between Hispanic and Anglo pastors, particularly on the topic of immigration.

7. **We continue to find it challenging to convert fans of Christian unity into investors in it.** Yet we continue to believe that the church in our city will be much stronger, and the city much healthier, when everyone is personally invested. One of several pieces we haven't figured out yet is how to help individuals take personal ownership and not simply say, "My church is a partner."

8. **We've largely been under the radar of the community beyond the church, except for the places where we've ventured in to serve.** Undoubtedly there will be some pushback coming at some point, and that's when our unity will be tested at new levels.

9. **That same pushback can be used by God just like persecution was in Acts 8.** It caused the Church to spread further and quicker than it likely would have otherwise. If we can maintain our core values—unity, collaboration, integrity, and service—then negative publicity intended for evil can be used by God to spread His love in ways that we could never match on our own. As light and darkness become less interspersed and more gathered together, both will grow in intensity. And when the two battle it out, light wins every single time.

About the Author

David Drum is a Tucson, Arizona native with a B.S. in Mechanical Engineering from the University of Arizona and an M.Div. from Trinity Lutheran Seminary. He served as the solo/lead pastor of Community of Hope Lutheran Church from 1990-2011. During that time the church underwent multiple transitions while maintaining unity throughout: from single to multiple staff; out of one denomination and into another; maintaining a Lutheran denominational heritage while also embracing the Charismatic Renewal movement. On August 1, 2011, he started as the full time Director of Church Development for 4Tucson, helping churches and pastors throughout Tucson work more closely together.

David has served as the president for Tucson Association of Evangelicals and Tucson Ministry Fellowship, on the national Board of Trustees and Board of Ministry for Lutheran Congregations in Mission for Christ (LCMC), and as the founder/leader for the Evangelical Renewal District of LCMC. He has published articles in Connections Magazine, Especially for Pastors Journal, and Sentinal Journal. *Coming To Conclusions Biblically* is a book he published in 1994 addressing the Lutheran denomination's struggles over topics relating to sexuality. Additionally several sermon series have been self published, including series on the book of Ruth and on the Beatitudes. He has presented workshops around the country through LCMC, and has taught at the Lutheran Bible School in Kiomboi, Tanzania.

Dave has been married to his beautiful wife Valerie for 25 years, and they have four children: Michael, Amy, Daniel and Emily. Dave is a unifier, a teacher, a Bible student, an avid Arizona Wildcat fan, a racquetball player, and has a pastor's heart.

ADDITIONAL READING

This list is by no means intended to be exhaustive, either on the topic of city transformation in general, or unity among Christians and the means of achieving that unity. Rather, it's a compilation of books and authors from whom I have personally benefited, many of which are cited in the chapters indicated.

CHAPTER 1 – ONE PASSIONATE FOCUS

With Christ in the School of Prayer (Peabody: Hendrickson Publishers, 2007), Andrew Murray. Murray has profound insights not only on prayer, but on the heart and nature of discipleship.

Morning by Morning (Uhrichsville: Barbour & Company, 1990), Charles Spurgeon. Spurgeon is the greatest artist with the English language I've ever encountered. Add in his profound insights into following Christ and this little devotional is a daily blessing.

When the Many are One: How to lay aside our differences and come together as the house of God (Lake Mary: Charisma House, 2009), Francis Frangipane. This is just one of many Frangipane works. I have heard Frangipane speak powerfully and eloquently many times on the importance of answering Jesus' John 17 prayer.

Mere Christianity (New York: Macmillan Publishing, 1952), C.S. Lewis. Lewis has shaped me more than any other author, and *Mere Christianity* is the book I've read more times than any other outside of the Bible itself. Lewis' goal in *Mere Christianity* is to teach only those truths that all Christians hold in common.

CHAPTER 2 – PAUL'S CITYWIDE ANALOGY

Missional Renaissance: Changing the Scorecard for the Church (San Francisco: Jossey-Bass, 2009), Reggie McNeal. This is one of many McNeal books on city transformation and changing trends within Christianity. His quote about the church becoming a "desalination plant" has been transformative for me personally, as well as foundational for our work in 4Tucson.

CHAPTER 4 – LEVEL 1: COMMON KINDNESS

Just Walk Across the Room: Simple steps pointing people to faith (Grand Rapids: Zondervan, 2006), Bill Hybels. This book does as much to enlist the whole congregation in the joy of evangelism as any I've read. Accompanying materials from the Willow Creek Association are equally valuable.

Conspiracy of Kindness (Ventura: Regal, 2003) and *101 Ways to Reach Your Community* (Colorado Springs: NavPress, 2001); both by Steve Sjogren. Together, these two books help whet the appetite for what a servant church can look like.

CHAPTER 5 – LEVEL 2: COMMON CAUSE

Mack and Leeann's Guide to Short Term Missions (Downers' Grove: InterVarsity Press, 2000), Mack and Leeann Stiles. This book was part of our team's training for our Tanzania trip. It's impossible to overstate the value of training, for the foreign mission trip itself and also for the reentry.

CHAPTER 6 – LEVEL 3: UNCOMMON LOVE

United and Ignited: Encountering God through Dynamic Corporate Prayer (Vancouver: L/P Press, 2012), Dennis Fuqua. Dennis has been the facilitator for all five of our three-day prayer summits, and truly knows about dynamic, life-giving, corporate prayer.

CHAPTER 7 – LEVEL 4: UNCOMMON HUMILITY

The Cross: Finding Life in Jesus' Death (Medina: Setting Captives Free Publishing, 2008), Mike Cleveland. This offers amazing biblical insight into the power and prevalence of the cross throughout the entire Bible. Don't let the packaging (typos, no page numbers, etc.) dissuade you – the cross wasn't pretty, either!

Joy Comes in the Mourning: and other blessings in disguise (Christian Publications, 1999), David Johnson with Tom Allen. The best discussion of the Beatitudes (Matthew 5:1-12) I've ever seen, and one of only two sermon series I ever preached twice in my own congregation.

Unchristian: What a new generation really thinks about Christianity... and why it matters (Grand Rapids: Baker Books, 2007), David Kinnaman. Valuable insights drawn from research about the culture in which we live.

Humility & Absolute Surrender (Peabody: Hendrickson Publishers, 2005), Andrew Murray. Humility (or the lack of it) is the limiting factor in our relationships, both with Christ and with one another.

Prayer (Minneapolis: Augsburg Publishing House, 1959), Ole Hallesby. This little classic on prayer draws from connecting prayer to humility. "We have faith enough when we in our helplessness turn to Jesus."

CHAPTER 9 – OUR COMMONWEALTH IN HEAVEN, HERE ON EARTH

Streams of Living Water: Celebrating the Great Traditions of Christian Faith (New York: HarperCollins Publishers, 1998), Richard Foster. Part of Foster's power as an author is how well versed he is in the breadth of Christian tradition. His books *Prayer; Money, Sex and Power* and his classic *Celebrating the Disciplines* all reflect and draw from the beauty of the whole body of Christ.

Empowered Evangelicals: Bringing Together the Best of the Evangelical and Charismatic Worlds (Ann Arbor: Servant Publications, 1995), Rich Nathan and Ken Wilson. Thankfully, the chasm between the Evangelical and Charismatic/Pentecostal worlds is being bridged; this book reflects and contributes to that reality.

When Heaven Invades Earth: A Practical Guide to a Life of Miracles (Shippensburg: Destiny Image Publishers, 2003), Bill Johnson. I love how direct and simple, yet profound and challenging, Johnson is, both as an author and as a speaker.

The Second Reformation: Reshaping the Church for the 21ˢᵗ Century (Touch Publications, 1997), William Beckham. This book helped launch our congregation's small group ministry, and reflects one aspect of the second reformation in which we find ourselves as a Christian church.

The Harvest (Fort Mill: MorningStar Publications, 2007), Rick Joyner. This twentieth anniversary edition reflects back on a series of visions Joyner received and first published. The book reads like a global newspaper, so uncanny and accurate is the vision that Joyner shares.

CHAPTER 10 – ONE CITY'S STRATEGIES

The Marriage Problem: How our Culture Has Weakened Families (New York: HarperCollins Publishers, 2002), James Q Wilson.

There are many books being published on city transformation. Here are a few of the most influential:

The Church of Irresistible Influence: Bridge-Building Stories to Help Reach Your Community (Grand Rapids: Zondervan, 2001), Robert Lewis.

To Transform a City: Whole Church, Whole Gospel, Whole City (Grand Rapids: Zondervan, 2010), Eric Swanson and Sam Williams.

The Externally Focused Church (Loveland: Group Publishing, 2004), Rick Rusaw and Eric Swanson.

Transformation: How Glocal (sic) *Churches Transform Lives and the World* (Grand Rapids: Zondervan, 2006), Bob Roberts, Jr.

Center Church: Doing Balanced, Gospel-Centered Ministry in Your City (Grand Rapids, Zondervan, 2012), Tim Keller.

CHAPTER 11 – ONE CITY'S STORIES

Experiencing God: How to Live the Full Adventure of Knowing and Doing the Will of God (Nashville: Broadman & Holman Publishers, 1994), Henry Blackaby and Claude King. Our whole approach to ministry in 4Tucson, summarized in the phrase "following God around town and taking notes," draws from the insights of Blackaby's classic.

ADDITIONAL SOURCES CITED (ALL FROM CHAPTER 6)

The Barna Group, "Unchurched Population Nears 100 Million in the U.S.", from http://www.barna.org/faith-spirituality/107-un-churched-population-nears-100-million-in-the-us?q=un-churched March 19, 2007

Church invitation statistics taken from Cornerstone Pastors Network website. http://www.ccnetonline.org/2010/08/16/useful-statistics-for-church-leaders/

American Religious Identification Survey statistic taken from U.S. News and World Report, "New Survey: Those With No Religion Fastest-Growing Tradition," by Dan Gilgoff http://www.usnews.com/news/blogs/god-and-country/2009/03/09/new-survey-those-with-no-religion-fastest-growing-tradition March 9, 2009

All the "One Another" Commandments in the New Testament

All verses from the New Revised Standard Version of the Bible

Love one another

John 13:34-35
I give you a new commandment, that you love one another. Just as I have loved you, you also should love one another. By this everyone will know that you are my disciples, if you have love for one another.

John 15:12
This is my commandment, that you love one another as I have loved you.

John 15:17
I am giving you these commands so that you may love one another.

Romans 12:10
Love one another with mutual affection; outdo one another in showing honor.

1 Thessalonians 4:9
Now concerning love of the brothers and sisters, you do not need to have anyone write to you, for you yourselves have been taught by God to love one another.

1 John 3:11

For this is the message you have heard from the beginning, that we should love one another.

1 John 3:23

And this is his commandment, that we should believe in the name of his Son Jesus Christ and love one another, just as he has commanded us.

1 John 4:7

Beloved, let us love one another, because love is from God; everyone who loves is born of God and knows God.

2 John 5

But now, dear lady, I ask you, not as though I were writing you a new commandment, but one we have had from the beginning, let us love one another.

Romans 13:8

Owe no one anything, except to love one another; for the one who loves another has fulfilled the law.

1 Thessalonians 3:12

And may the Lord make you increase and abound in love for one another and for all, just as we abound in love for you.

2 Thessalonians 1:3

We must always give thanks to God for you, brothers and sisters, as is right, because your faith is growing abundantly, and the love of everyone of you for one another is increasing.

1 Peter 1:22

Now that you have purified your souls by your obedience to the truth so that you have genuine mutual love, love one another deeply from the heart.

1 John 4:11-12
Beloved, since God loved us so much, we also ought to love one another. No one has ever seen God; if we love one another, God lives in us, and his love is perfected in us.

ENCOURAGE ONE ANOTHER

1 Thessalonians 4:18
Therefore encourage one another with these words.

1 Thessalonians 5:11
Therefore encourage one another and build up each other, as indeed you are doing.

Romans 1:12
Or rather so that we may be mutually encouraged by each other's faith, both yours and mine.

Romans 14:19
Let us then pursue what makes for peace and for mutual upbuilding.

Hebrews 10:24-25
And let us consider how to provoke one another to love and good deeds, not neglecting to meet together, as is the habit of some, but encouraging one another, and all the more as you see the Day approaching.

BEAR WITH ONE ANOTHER

Ephesians 4:1-3
I therefore, the prisoner in the Lord, beg you to lead a life worthy of the calling to which you have been called, with all humility and gentleness, with patience, bearing with one another in love, making every effort to maintain the unity of the Spirit in the bond of peace.

Galatians 6:2
Bear one another's burdens, and in this way you will fulfill the law of Christ.

Colossians 3:13

Bear with one another and, if anyone has a complaint against another, forgive each other; just as the Lord has forgiven you, so you also must forgive.

Members of one another

Romans 12:5

So we, who are many, are one body in Christ, and individually we are members one of another.

1 Corinthians 12:24-26

But God has so arranged the body, giving the greater honor to the inferior member, that there may be no dissension within the body, but the members may have the same care for one another. If one member suffers, all suffer together with it; if one member is honored, all rejoice together with it.

Ephesians 4:25

So then, putting away falsehood, let all of us speak the truth to our neighbors, for we are members of one another.

Humility, serving one another

John 13:14

So if I, your Lord and Teacher, have washed your feet, you also ought to wash one another's feet.

Galatians 5:13-15

For you were called to freedom, brothers and sisters; only do not use your freedom as an opportunity for self-indulgence, but through love become slaves to one another. For the whole law is summed up in a single commandment, "You shall love your neighbor as yourself." If, however, you bite and devour one another, take care that you are not consumed by one another.

Ephesians 5:21
Be subject to one another out of reverence for Christ.

Philippians 2:3
Do nothing from selfish ambition or conceit, but in humility regard others as better than yourselves.

1 Peter 5:5
In the same way, you who are younger must accept the authority of the elders. And all of you must clothe yourselves with humility in your dealings with one another, for "God opposes the proud, but gives grace to the humble."

HOSPITALITY, CARING FOR AND WELCOMING ONE ANOTHER

Romans 15:7
Welcome one another, therefore, just as Christ has welcomed you, for the glory of God.

1 Corinthians 11:33
So then, my brothers and sisters, when you come together to eat, wait for one another.

1 Corinthians 12:24-26
But God has so arranged the body, giving the greater honor to the inferior member, that there may be no dissension within the body, but the members may have the same care for one another. If one member suffers, all suffer together with it; if one member is honored, all rejoice together with it.

Ephesians 4:32
And be kind to one another, tenderhearted, forgiving one another, as God in Christ has forgiven you.

1 Thessalonians 5:15
See that none of you repays evil for evil, but always seek to do good to one another and to all.

1 Peter 4:9
Be hospitable to one another without complaining.

Romans 16:16
Greet one another with a holy kiss. All the churches of Christ greet you.

1 Corinthians 16:20
All the brothers and sisters send greetings. Greet one another with a holy kiss.

2 Corinthians 13:12
Greet one another with a holy kiss. All the saints greet you.

1 Peter 5:14
Greet one another with a kiss of love. Peace to all of you who are in Christ.

BE AT PEACE WITH ONE ANOTHER

Mark 9:50
Salt is good; but if salt has lost its saltiness, how can you season it? Have salt in yourselves, and be at peace with one another.

Romans 12:16
Live in harmony with one another; do not be haughty, but associate with the lowly; do not claim to be wiser than you are.

Romans 15:4-5
For whatever was written in former days was written for our instruction, so that by steadfastness and by the encouragement of the scriptures we might have hope. May the God of steadfastness and encouragement grant you to live in harmony with one another, in accordance with Christ Jesus.

CONFESS TO AND FORGIVE ONE ANOTHER

1 John 1:6-7
If we say that we have fellowship with him while we are walking in darkness, we lie and do not do what is true; but if we walk in the light as he himself is in the light, we have fellowship with one another, and the blood of Jesus his Son cleanses us from all sin.

James 5:16
Therefore confess your sins to one another, and pray for one another, so that you may be healed. The prayer of the righteous is powerful and effective.

Ephesians 4:32
And be kind to one another, tenderhearted, forgiving one another, as God in Christ has forgiven you.

Colossians 3:13
Bear with one another and, if anyone has a complaint against another, forgive each other; just as the Lord has forgiven you, so you also must forgive.

PRAY FOR ONE ANOTHER

James 5:16
Therefore confess your sins to one another, and pray for one another, so that you may be healed. The prayer of the righteous is powerful and effective.

TEACH ONE ANOTHER

Romans 15:14
I myself feel confident about you, my brothers and sisters, that you yourselves are full of goodness, filled with all knowledge, and able to instruct one another.

Colossians 3:15-17
And let the peace of Christ rule in your hearts, to which indeed you were called in the one body. And be thankful. Let the word of Christ dwell in you richly; teach and admonish one another in all wisdom; and with gratitude in your hearts sing psalms, hymns, and spiritual songs to God. And whatever you do, in word or deed, do everything in the name of the Lord Jesus, giving thanks to God the Father through him.

PROHIBITIONS – DON'T DO THIS TO ONE ANOTHER

John 6:43
Jesus answered them, "Do not complain among yourselves."

Romans 14:13
Let us therefore no longer pass judgment on one another, but resolve instead never to put a stumbling block or hindrance in the way of another.

1 Corinthians 7:4-5
For the wife does not have authority over her own body, but the husband does; likewise the husband does not have authority over his own body, but the wife does. Do not deprive one another except perhaps by agreement for a set time, to devote yourselves to prayer, and then come together again, so that Satan may not tempt you because of your lack of self-control.

Galatians 5:26
Let us not become conceited, competing against one another, envying one another.

Colossians 3:9-10
Do not lie to one another, seeing that you have stripped off the old self with its practices and have clothed yourselves with the new self, which is being renewed in knowledge according to the image of its creator.

Titus 3:3
For we ourselves were once foolish, disobedient, led astray, slaves to various passions and pleasures, passing our days in malice and envy, despicable, hating one another.

James 4:11
Do not speak evil against one another, brothers and sisters. Whoever speaks evil against another or judges another, speaks evil against the law and judges the law; but if you judge the law, you are not a doer of the law but a judge.

James 5:9
Beloved, do not grumble against one another, so that you may not be judged. See, the Judge is standing at the doors!

READY TO ADD *YOUR PIECE* TO THE PUZZLE?

Are you an investor in visible, Christian unity in your city? Here are a few steps you can take to add to the picture Jesus is painting in your city.

FOR YOU PERSONALLY...

- Make the Scripture passages in this book (especially John 17, 1 Corinthians 12, and Ephesians 4) a regular part of your prayer life.

- Go back through the practical investment steps in Section 2, and pick out at least one from each chapter. Pray and put it into practice.

- God likely will give you additional insight as you grow through the various levels of unity. Go to www.jesussurprisingstrategy. com and share what God's showing you. Everyone benefits!

- Does your city have a developing strategy for Christian unity? Do some investigating. Some places to start are www.missionamerica.org and www.gospelmovements.org. If you're in Southern Arizona, dive into what God's doing there through www.4tucson.com.

FOR YOU WITH OTHERS...

- Did other people come to mind as you read *Jesus' Surprising Strategy?* Encourage them to buy a copy—or give them one as a gift. Copies can be ordered at www.jesussurprisingstrategy.com or through Amazon and other selected outlets.

- Are you part of a small group through your church? Read through the book together and evaluate how your group is doing at loving one another.

- If you're not currently part of a small group, start one and use this book as one source of material.

- Have the leadership group of your church read through the book together and evaluate how your congregation is doing at loving one another. Use the Additional Reading section for plenty of other resources.

- What domain are you most passionate about (see Chapter 10)? Do you know some others who share that passion? Invite them to work through the book together.

- If you're a pastor, encourage some other pastors you know to read *Jesus' Surprising Strategy* and put it into practice. Or use the material in Section Two to evaluate how much of Jesus' John 17 prayer is being answered in your city.

If you would like to have Dave come and share on this topic with your congregation or group, he is an experienced and engaging speaker and would be glad to consider your request. Contact him at www.jesussurprisingstrategy.com.